York and its Railways 1839-1950

Paul Chrystal

An earlt 20th Century picture of York Railway Workers. Photo © *York Press.*

Stenlake Publishing Ltd.

First Published in the United Kingdom, 2015
Stenlake Publishing Limited
54-58 Mill Square, Catrine, KA5 6RD
www.stenlake.co.uk

ISBN 9781840337082

ACKNOWLEDGEMENTS

Thanks to John Clarke for permission to use the images from his Railway Wonders of the World, Famous Railway Centres 1: York website [From part 12, published 18 April 1935]. Colin Weir of York Railway InstituteIan Drake of YAYAS for the photo on page 33; BR North Eastern Magazine and Steve Lewis at York Press.

John Clarke's pictures. xxx

FURTHER READING

Anonymous Diary of a Nursing Sister on the Western Front (1915), (Edinburgh)
Appleby, K. (1993) *Britain's Rail Super Centres: York* (Shepperton)
Arnold, A.J. (2004), *George Hudson: The Rise and Fall of the Railway King*, (London)
Bailey, B. (1995), *George Hudson*, (Stroud)
Beaumont, R. (2003), *The Railway King*, (London)
Bell, R. *Twenty Five Years of the North Eastern Railway 1898-1922*
British Railways Press Office (1943), *Facts About British Railways in Wartime 1943*
Burgess, N. (2011), *The Lost Railways of Yorkshire's North Riding* (Catrine)
Chrystal, P. (2013), *The Rowntree Family of York* (Pickering)
(2012) *York Industries Through Time* (Stroud)
(2011) *A History of Chocolate in York* (Barnsley)
Cole, B. (1994) *York Through The Eyes of the Railways* (York)
Crump, H. (1947), *By Rail to Victory: The Story of the LNER in Wartime* (London)
Darsley, R.R. (1994) *Industrial Railways of York* (Birmingham)
Duckham, B.F. (1956) *Economic Development of York, 1830-1914* (diss. Manchester University)
Edgington, J. (2002), *Trains from York* (Penryn)
Fawcett, B. (2011), *George Townsend Andrews of York – 'The Railway Architect'* (York)
(2006), *The North Eastern Railway's Two Palaces of Business* (York)
(1995), *A History of the York - Scarborough Railway* (Beverley)
Feinstein, C.H. (ed), (1983) *York 1831 -1981: 150 Years of Scientific Endeavour and Social Change* (York)
Fowkes, J.W. (1958), *Economic and Social Development of York, 1830-1870* (diss. Liverpool University)
Hennessey, R.A.S. (1970) *The Electric Railway that Never Was: York – Newcastle 1919* (Newcastle)
Hoole, K. *Railway Stations of the North East* (Newton Abbott)
(1983) *Railway Centres: York* (Nottingham)
(1976) *The Railways of York* (Clapham, Lancaster)
Jenkinson, D. (1981) *Palaces on Wheels: Royal Carriages at the National Railway Museum* (Tunbridge Wells)
Johnson, J.P. (1996), *Hudson, Goodrick and Glory, York History 1996*
Kessler, L. *The York Blitz 1942* (York)
Lambert, R. S (1934), *The Railway King 1800–1871, A Study of George Hudson and the Business Morals of his Times* (London)
Langham, R. (2013) *The North East Railway in the First World War* (Stroud)
Mitchell, V, (2003). *Branch Line to the Derwent Valley, including the Foss Islands Branch.* (Midhurst)
Murray, H. (1989) *Opportunity of Leisure: The History of the York Railway Institute, 1889-1989* (York)
Myler, C. (1995), *The Life and Times of York Carriage Works 1884-1995* (York)
Peacock, A.J. (1988-1989) *George Hudson Vols 1 and 2*
(1981) *George Leeman and York Politics 1833–1880* in Feinstein (1983)
(1974) *George Hudson and the Historians, York History 1974*
(1971), *George Hudson of York*, (Clapham, Lancashire)
Rankin, S. (1984), *This is York: The Story of a Station* (York)
Reading, S.J. (1967), *The Derwent Valley Light Railway*
Rubinstein, D. (2010) *War Comes to York, Summer 1914* (York)
Sanderson, E. *Railway Memories of York* (Bellcode Books)
Thompson, A.R. (1994) *British Railways Past & Present: North Yorkshire* (Kettering)
Tomlinson, W.W. (1967) *North Eastern Railway* (Newton Abbott)
Vaughan, A. (1997), *Railwaymen, Politics and Money*, (London)
Visit to the North-Eastern Railway Carriage and Wagon Works at York, 13th July, 1920 (1920), *Journal of the Institution of Locomotive Engineers* 10 (44): 308–310
Winchester, C., ed. (1935), *Famous Railway Centres 1: York, Railway Wonders of the World*, pp. 375–380

CONTENTS

Aerial view of York Staton.

PREFACE

York has been a major UK railway centre since 1839 when the first trains came and went from the city. Its future as a hub was allegedly ensured when the wily George Hudson – the 'Railway King' – convinced a compliant George Stephenson, apparently, to *"mak all t'railways cum t' York"*.

Stephenson's decision had a huge impact on the city, boosting it socially, culturally, commercially and industrially – an impact which has resonated in York and the surrounding region for some 150 years and still resounds today.

It contributed to the emergence of York's global confectionery industry and a whole host of other commercial successes. York became the headquarters of the mighty NER and the carriage works and, later, the National Railway Museum and its unparalleled exhibits and railway research facilities; York did sterling work during the First World War war effort; it also enjoyed the less welcome attentions of the Luftwaffe with dramatic and tragic consequences in the Second World War.

This is the first book for many years to provide a detailed assessment of York and its early railways, charting the commercial, cultural and social impact on the city and surrounding region, and analysing its role in a national context.

The history and development of the railway industry here is covered with chapters on the carriage works, local industrial railways, the three York stations and NER, the crafty or cautious Georges Hudson and Leeman, ambulance trains in the Great War, the destructive Baedeker air raid, the National Railway Museum and station hotels.

An aerial view of York's magnificent station, expansive goods yards and the Station Hotel, *c.* 1928.

NER poster promoting historic York in all its glory. This particular copy graces a wall in the men's toilet in The York Tap on York Station, that marvellous conversion of a uniform store.

York Station in the early 20th century.

The Railways Around York

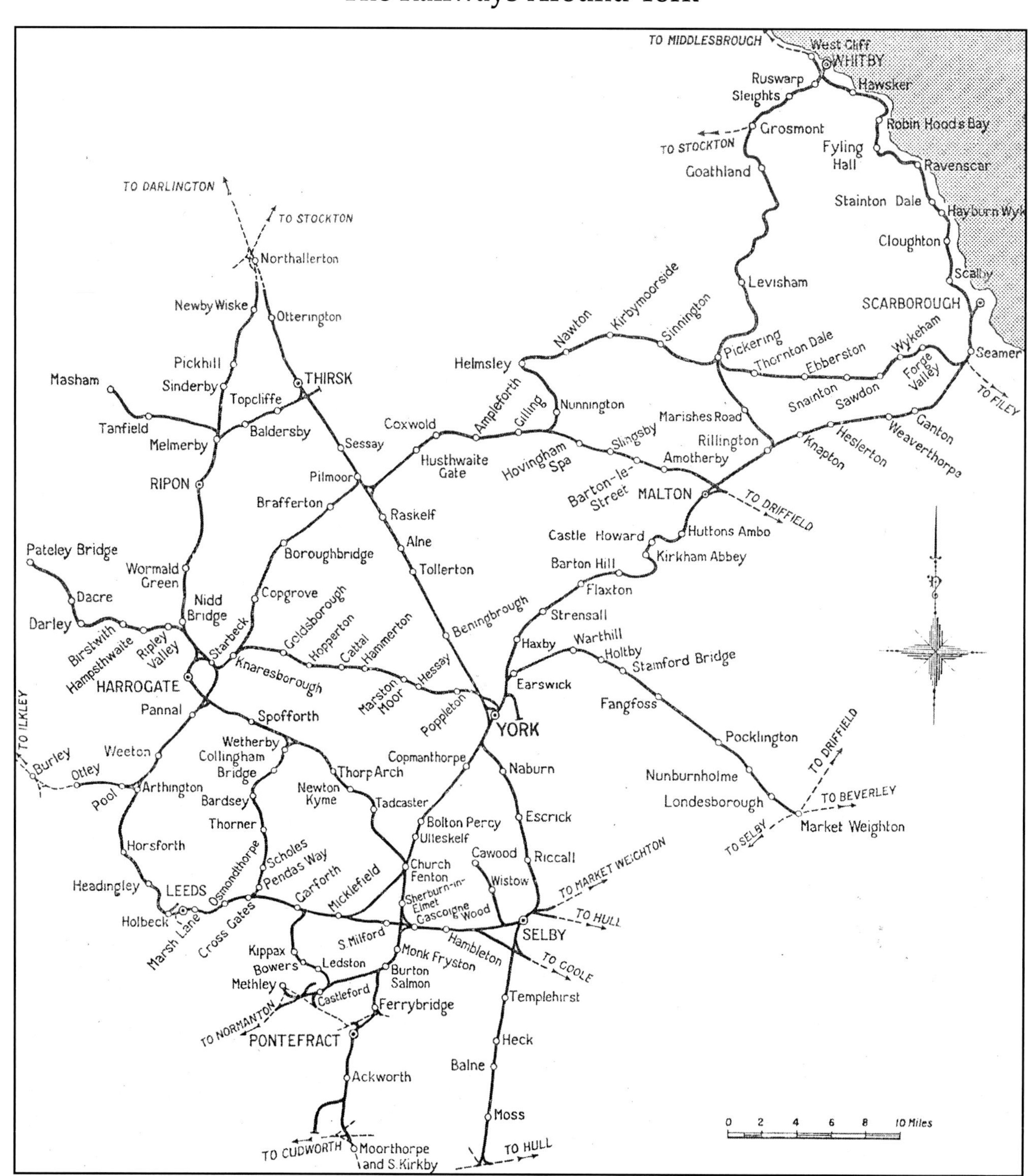

YORK BEFORE THE RAILWAYS CAME

In the second half of the 14th century York, on account of its thriving cloth trade and the ancillary industries associated with it, was described as 'the foremost industrial town in the North of England.' This did not last: the trade in cloth declined to such a degree that a visitor to the city in the 17th century, Thomas Fuller, disparagingly but wittily remarked that 'the foreign trade is like their river...low and flat.'

According to Francis Drake too, in his *Eboracum: or the History and Antiquities of the City of York*, York in the 18th century had precious little industry: the only real commercial activity was butter exports, corn and wine trading. Defoe, in *A Tour Through the Whole Island of Great Britain* agreed: ' here is no trade... except such as depends upon the confluence of the gentry.' This was due to some extent both to the high price in York of coal which had to be shipped from the coalfields of the West Riding, and to the restrictive, exclusive attitude of the local Merchant Adventurers and their insistence that the freedom regulations, whereby all traders had to be freemen of the City, be rigorously and inflexibly observed. Moreover, up until 1827 when a judgement went against them, it seems that only members of the Merchant Adventurers' Company could carry out trade in imported goods.

Were pricey coal and exclusive, monopolistic Adventurers all to blame for this malaise? The high price of coal would only really affect any heavy industry (of which there was very little anyway) and the strictures imposed by the Merchant Adventurers would not have impeded development and progress amongst established manufacturers and traders. Instead, we can probably lay a good part of the cause of the industrial anathema at the door of the Corporation whose medieval constitution, financial straits and general lack of enterprise did little to attract, promote or sustain industry or commerce at a significant level.

So what sort of city did the fledgling rail industry find itself in in 1839? If the 1775 register of freemen is to be believed only 600 enfranchised members were actually engaged in manufacturing while many more were merchants, grocers or innkeepers: York it seems was now destined just to function as a parochial market town supplying its own and the surrounding area's basic needs, goods and services and

Bustling King's Staith on the Ouse.

The confluence of the Ouse and the Foss at Blue Bridge.

those of the Church and the gentry who frequented the city. Communications were good by road or river and facilitated the importation of coal (98,000 tons annually in the 1830s) and the export of agricultural produce, for example to Leeds, which, in the same period amounted to 110,000 sheep and 53,000 cattle and 30,000 tons of grain. But by the end of the century the substantial butter trade had declined and York, though still a major ecclesiastical centre, was no longer the magnet, the place to be seen, for the northern gentry it had once been; the traditional trade catering for these people suffered as a result.

The Rivers Foss and Ouse were vital to what there was of an industrial base in York. The Ouse was crucial to York from earliest times, right through the Roman and Viking occupations and into the Middle Ages, making York an important port. Roman jetties, wharves and warehouses have been excavated on the river banks, indicating that water-borne transport and trade was especially important from Roman times. Evidence of Irish and German boats dates from around 1125. A ship's figurehead in Stonegate and the timbers from which many of the city's buildings were built, indicate York's history as a viable port. In 1069 William the Conqueror dammed the River Foss near to its confluence with the Ouse to create a moat around the castle; this caused the river to flood upstream and form a large fetid lake known as the King's Pool or the King's Fish Pond. King's Pool was an integral feature of the city's inner defences during the Middle Ages as the marsh was virtually impassable and explains why there is no city wall between Layerthorpe Postern and the Red Tower. Foss Bridge, at the end of Walmgate, dates from 1811 and replaces a 1403 stone bridge and a wooden one before that. It was a commercial centre of some note: the fish shambles were here as was the Saturday pig market (the tethering rings still exist) and the goose fair.

However, the only real developments in the 18th and 19th centuries were with small industries such as leather making (in tanneries in Walmgate on the Foss and at Marygate on the Ouse) and comb and horn breaking which was active mainly around Hornpot Lane off Petergate; the combmakers worked in ivory and tortoiseshell as well as in horn. One of the more successful comb companies was Forbes and Fothergill near Toft Green; Joseph Rougier was also successful in Tanner Row – and was descended from a Huguenot family of wigmakers and hairdressers; other combmakers included B. Lund in St Andrewgate. Glass was made by Prince and Prest's Fishergate Glass Works established in 1797, and flour milling was in North Street and Skeldergate. 1780 saw the establishment of Bleasdale Ltd, manufacturing and wholesale chemists behind Colliergate while other pharmaceutical and chemical manufacturers included Wright and Prest in Pavement, Edward Wallis & Son in Bedern and Thomas Bishop at North Street Postern. Breweries were run by the Wormald family and Thomas Hartley. A modest amount of shipbuilding came and quickly went after the construction of six brigantines outside Skeldergate Postern for butter exports around 1770, to be followed by a further three brigantines in 1776 and three more in 1781, 1783 and 1797. Heavy

industries like iron making were limited to Stodhart in Coney Street producing lamps and kitchen tools, John Spence in Bootham Bar, Masterman and Gibson in Manor Yard and Prince and Holmes on the River Foss.

The Ouse at Marygate Tower, unloading supplies, probably coal, for on-shipment by horse and cart to St Mary's Abbey.

The 1841 census gives the following figures for the industries that were of any significance: glass making: 54 persons employed in three firms with an average workforce of eighteen persons; flax and linen manufacture: 118 employees in eight firms with an average of fifteen; iron making: 25 firms, average four; chemists and druggists: 76 workers in 38 firms averaging two people per firm; 107 comb manufacturers in nine firms averaging twelve people per firm.

The seeds of York's reputation as a social centre started with the ubiquitous coffee house and went on to flourish later in the posh Assembly Rooms. People came to York to socialise. Coffee houses abounded in York from 1669 – there are at least 30 recorded amongst which were Parker's in Minster Yard – next to a bowling alley as shown on Horsley's 1896 map, the Garrick in Low Petergate, Wombwell and Wink's, Harrison's in Petergate and later Nessgate; Iveson's, also in Petergate; Duke's near to the Ouse Bridge; and Brigg's on the corner of Stonegate and Coffee Yard – as well as William Tuke's roasting house. As one of 31 York tea dealers in 1823 and importers of tea, coffee and chocolate the Tuke's were the sole holders in the north of England of a licence which permitted the processing of coffee beans and the sale of roasted coffee, tea and chocolate. It is reasonable to assume that once drinking chocolate and cocoa became popular then, as elsewhere, they would have been added to the list of beverages available in York's coffee shops.

At the beginning of the 19th century the population of York (municipal borough) was 16,846; by the end of that century this more than doubled to 54,742 with the biggest annual increase (26%) coming in the 1840s soon after the arrival of the railways. Towns and cities like Leeds, Huddersfield and Bradford benefitting more directly from the Industrial Revolution showed much bigger increases, but the Industrial Revolution largely passed York by. Indeed, in 1851 York had twice as many domestic servants on its books as the other three, and an above national average number of small artisan trades and shopkeepers: one shop for every 55 people; 2,800 people or seventeen per cent of the city's workforce were in service (for women the figure was 75%) and a further 91 (5 $^1/_2$%) in "hospitality" – hotels and inns. By comparison, manufacturing accounted for 3,170 persons or just over 19% of the economically active. Furthermore, at the dawn of the 19th century, York was England's sixteenth largest city and the

Foss river trade in winter.

Iced up river traffic on the Ouse at the turn of the 20th century. Terry's first factory at Clementhorpe can be seen on the right bank, belching smoke. It later moved to Bishopthorpe Road.

fourth largest in Yorkshire after Leeds, Sheffield and Hull. By the end of the century it was the 41st largest in the country and in Yorkshire had been surpassed by Bradford, Middlesbrough, Halifax and Huddersfield.

Before the railways many goods were transported in and out of the city on the River Ouse and the River Foss. Archaeological discoveries including those Roman jetties, wharves and warehouses on the banks of the Foss would suggest that river transport and trade was a vital part of the city's commercial activity from the 1st century AD. Eight hundred years later the Vikings introduced shipbuilding and navigation expertise, making their York a thriving trading port and commercial centre. Imports and exports were facilitated by access to the North Sea along the Ouse: archaeological finds from Viking York are truly international and include amber and furs from Scandinavia, silk from China and the Middle East, copper alloy pins from Ireland, a cowrie shell from the Red Sea and pottery from Germany.

By the 14th century the city was England's richest city after London, and the clannish Merchant Adventurers was the most affluent guild. York's merchants exported wool, grain and textiles and imported olive oil, figs and raisins. The steady growth in the size of ships, however, meant that in the 16th century many sea-going ships could no longer navigate York's rivers; York was commercially isolated while the West Riding thrived at York's expense. York's trading importance inevitably declined.

THE RAILWAYS COME TO YORK

The industrialists and businessmen of York, in common with those in other towns and cities, were anxious to share in the commercial opportunities the like of which had benefitted towns close to the Stockton & Darlington railway from 1825. The year 1826 saw York people making a case for a link to York from the Croft branch just south of Darlington via Northallerton and Easingwold. Liverpool and Manchester showed how intercity links could work, in 1830. Nothing much happened in York, though, until 1833 when a company was formed to connect York and Leeds, and then the other industrial towns and cities of the West Riding. The favoured route went via Tadcaster, reaching Leeds via the emerging Leeds and Selby Railway. To York, though, the ultimate prize was to be an integral part of the London – Scotland route. There was talk too, but only talk, of a York link to join up with the Whitby – Pickering line, but the diverse interested parties involved achieved nothing. All the plans were diverted into a siding until the intervention of the charismatic charlatan George Hudson who, characteristically, faced the issue head on and, true to his word, made most, if not all, of the railways go through York.

White's 1840 Directory too had high hopes for the future:

> 'The formation of railways to open a better communication with the West of Yorkshire and the North and South of England, are in progress and with these improved modes of transit for goods, it is to be hoped that the trade of York will improve.'

In the event, the railways did not lead to a large expansion of industry, even though six main line companies were soon calling at York. They did, however, bring their own opportunities for employment and the obvious benefit in communication with the rest of the country, and indeed with the world, as access to Hull and other east coast ports was improved immeasurably.

In what sort of city did the railway industry find itself in? York industries in 1851 were still small fry by any comparison. The glassworks in Fishergate was ailing and was taken over by Joseph Spence, a Quaker analytical chemist, James Meek and Thomas Spence to become the successful York Flint Glass Company; it employed 223 men turning out chemists' jars, railway lamps, beetle and wasp traps, cake shades, cruets and Daffy's Alexir glasses. The metal industry was shared between John Walker with 52 men, Edwin Thompson, 48 men and William Knapton, eighteen men. George Steward's comb manufacturing had 30 men while E. Steward had eighteen in the same industry; William Hebden, linen maker, had a workforce of 35 men, seven boys and one woman. In 1823 there were nine toy and

Outside the Black Swan on race day – nothing much has changed although the Black Swan is long gone.

0-6-0T No. 1167 at York Station.

The Aerolite in its second rebuild as a 2-2-4T under the walls at York. It was built in Leeds in 1851. Locomotives were often displayed here before integration in the collection in the Queen Street railway museum.

household trinket manufacturers including John Barber of Coney Street, John Bell in Stonegate and John Jameson of College Street.

Chemicals, flour milling and printing were the only other industries of any size with 150 chemical workers at the end of the century and 98 millers, mainly at Leetham's in Wormald Cut in 1891 rising to 600 in 1911; there were nearly 500 employed in the printing and publishing trade, also in 1891. Printing had been established in York since the 15th century and by 1750 there were four printing houses in the city. The largest of these companies was run by the Quaker William Alexander from 1811 in Lower Ousegate, later to be taken over in 1865 by another Quaker, William Sessions who moved the firm to Coney Street in 1894. Alexander was following in the tradition of Thomas Gent, eccentric author and printer, who operated out of Coffee Yard from 1724 and published the first local newspaper and scores of chap books. Ben Johnson & Co Ltd was established as a lithographic printer by Johnson and John Lancaster specialising in railway timetables and other jobs associated with the railways. Newspapers obviously also provided employment in the shape of the Whig *York Courant*, set up by Caesar Ward in the 1750s – Ward was also the publisher of the first edition of Laurence Sterne's *The Life and Opinions of Tristram Shandy* – the *York Daily Herald* (which changed from a weekly in 1874 and absorbed the *Courant* in 1848) and the 1882 *York Evening Press*, now the morning *York Press*.

Apart from Bleasdale's in the chemical and drug making industry there was also Raimes and Company from 1818 in Micklegate and Henry Richardson and Company, fertilizer makers founded in 1824 at Skeldergate Postern in Clementhorpe. John Walker's iron foundry was very successful and received Queen Victoria's royal warrant in 1847. In 1850 they won the contract to supply the extensive railings and gates for the British Museum and for the Sandringham Estate. In addition, much of their work was in gates and railings for the many country houses around York and at British embassies and foreign government buildings abroad, an example being the Botanical Gardens in Mauritius. The Adams Patent Sewage Lift Company Ltd was established in Peaseholme Green in 1887 to make sanitary equipment; they merged in 1919 with the 1885 iron foundry, G.W. Kirk, their biggest supplier.

Another specialist company was Thomas Cooke, an entrepreneurial optician who went on to make quality sundials, microscopes and telescopes from 1837. The firm moved from Stonegate to the Buckingham Works on Bishophill in 1856 and was run by Cooke's two sons after his death in 1868: by the end of the century they had diversified into clock making and employed 500 workers. Cooke also invented a revolutionary steam car which carried fifteen passengers at a speed of fifteen mph but which was outlawed by the Road Act; this prohibited vehicles which travelled above four mph; his sons invented the pneumatic despatch system.

The development of flour milling in York was particularly important: Henry Leetham set up his milling industry in Hungate on the banks of the River Foss in 1850, replacing his old steam mills with state of the art Hungarian steel rollers for corn milling. In 1888 he flexed his industrial muscle by threatening to relocate to Hull if the City Corporation refused to enlarge the lock at the entry to the Foss at Castle Mills. This they duly did and grain replaced coal as the biggest river cargo. At the same time Leetham negotiated very favourable terms for the transportation of their goods. Leetham went on to build his landmark five storey warehouse in 1896 on Wormald's Cut with its nine storey castellated water tower linked to the Hungate Mill by bridges. At the time it was one of the largest mills in Europe with operations in Hull, Newcastle and Cardiff as well as York, all showing handsome profits of around £50,000 per year with a wholesale customer base of around 9,000.

NER 1244 *en route* to the second York Station, inside the city walls.

Two more NER locomotives at York in 1905.

Two early views of the Scarborough Bridge. The second, a watercolour, shows the cast iron bridge carrying the Scarborough line over the Ouse. Health & Safety was nowhere in evidence when it was designed to incorporate a public footpath between the two tracks accessed by an internal stair-case between the two abutments reached by the side arches.

Steam train crossing Scarborough Bridge in the 1920s.

The confectionery trade had started to emerge as a major employer – for women as well as for men: by 1851 Joseph Terry employed 127 workers in St Helen's Square and Thomas Craven was working with 63 men and 60 boys; by the end of the century the firm employed over 200. Craven's production was in Coppergate – roughly where the Jorvik Viking Centre now stands along with additional properties in Coney Street and Foss Islands Road. When Mary Craven took over, there were around 200 workers; by 1908 this had increased to 800 – a sizeable business by York standards. In addition to production, packaging, despatch and marketing there were four Craven's retail shops in the city. One of these, Craven's Mary Ann Sweet Shop, was in the Shambles and featured a sweet museum on the first floor where visitors could see 150 years of the '*Art, Trade, Mystery and Business of the Confectioner*'. York's tourist industry was on the up. There was also the York Confectionery Company founded in 1867 in Fossgate, then moving to Fenwick Street off Bishopthorpe Road, specialising in candied peel and red and white mint rock for the seaside market. York Confectionery Company was owned by a man called Henderson; little is known about him apart from that he suffered from dyspnea, shortness of breath, and his factory became known as Puffy's as a result. He went bankrupt in 1909. In 1879 Rowntrees employed 100 workers; this increased to 893 in 1894 and by 1909 had reached 4,066.

George Hudson, the chairman of the North Midland Railway, was the York – Leeds line's chief advocate. He had already commissioned George Stephenson to build a line between Leeds and Derby. The railways came to the city on May 29th 1839, as the York & North Midland Railway, with the first services to London a year later; one of the world's first inter-city lines. The route, however, was somewhat circuitous, taking passengers via Derby and Rugby. The railway was linked to the Leeds, Selby & Hull line at South Milford.

May 29th was a massive day for York. After a 'breakfast of the most sumptuous description' at the Guildhall, a large crowd processed from the Mansion House to the temporary station in Queen Street where the inaugural train waited. It was made up of eighteen coaches pulled by two engines, appropriately named *The Lowther* and *The York and Leeds*, both built by Robert Stephenson. It pulled out of York at 1.06 pm arriving at South Milford fourteen and a half miles away 36 minutes later. At 2.23 it set off back to York arriving at 3.04 pm. More extravagance and partying followed with a dinner and ball at which Hudson presided and Stephenson gave an address.

After a series of extensions the York – London service began in July 1840 with four trains up and three down, departing 7.30 am; 9.00 am; 12.30 pm and 4.00 pm arriving Euston Square via Derby, Leicester and Rugby, or Birmingham and Rugby at 6.45 pm, 7.00 pm, 11.30 pm and 5.30 am respectively. Return journeys left Euston Square at 6.00 am, 9.30 am and 8.30 pm. The fastest journey was the 9.30 am down taking nine hours 45 minutes.

Thomas Cooke's famous steam car – banned from the road and adapted to the Ouse.
Photo courtesy of AJ Munro of Vickers Instruments.

THE GEORGE HUDSON FACTOR

Off the Rails! Leech's *Punch* cartoon of 1849.

'The Railway King', George Hudson, was prominent in York's development as a major railway city; his (probably apocryphal) advice to George Stephenson was to make York, his adopted city, a hub: *'Mak all t'railways cum t'York'*. Forget Leeds, he must have argued, the popular choice at the time. Stephenson took that advice and with the lines came a significant boon to local industry and tourism. Although the industrial landscape did not change in anything like the way many people expected, the visitors flocked in and still flock to this day.

Hudson was born in 1800 at Howsham some twelve miles to the north east of York, later in life earning the sobriquet, 'Railway King', from Sidney Smith, the author, wit and Anglican cleric. He is also owed credit for his part in establishing the line from King's Cross to Edinburgh Waverley although his memory will always be stained with illegal financial malpractice, chicanery and a distinct lack of transparency in his commercial and political dealings.

By age eight Hudson was an orphan raised by elder brothers; seven years later he left Howsham to make his fortune in York where he undertook an apprenticeship at Bell & Nicholson, a firm of drapers at 1 College Street near the Minster. In 1820 he completed his time and was taken on as a tradesman. 1821 was a big year for Hudson: he gained a share in the business and married Nicholson's daughter Elizabeth; they had seven children together. When Bell retired, the firm became Nicholson & Hudson, and by 1827 the company was the largest business in York. In 1827 Hudson had the good fortune to be left £30,000 by his great-uncle Matthew Botrill. Hudson had been rather over solicitous in caring for Botrill during his illness, a fact which has raised suspicions regarding the legality of the bequest. Reflecting on his life when in exile in France, Hudson concluded 'it was the very worst thing that could have happened to me. It let me into the railways and all my misfortunes since'. He used the money to inveigle and insinuate himself into the York establishment. The Hudsons moved from College Street to a house in the more salubrious Monkgate.

In April 1832 the Board of Health was reconstituted under the *Cholera Prevention Act*, forcing local authorities to pay for improvements once cholera had been confirmed. Around this time Joseph Rowntree, Samuel Tuke and George Hudson joined the York Board. Hudson distinguished himself by visiting the sick during the cholera outbreak in 1832, during which he had a major altercation with the Liberal Joseph Rowntree over how the parish rate should be spent on cholera control, and how an extension to the cholera hospital might be paid for. Hudson converted from being a Methodist and a Dissenter to a High Church Tory, becoming treasurer of the York Conservative Party in 1832. In 1833 joint stock country banks were able to conduct their business in the City of London; Hudson had a prominent role in the establishment of the York Union Banking Company with Glyn's as their London agent.

In 1835 he was elected to York City Council and became alderman in 1837 and Lord Mayor for 1837-8; this event was marked by an extravagant banquet in honour of the Archbishop of York, followed by a ball to honour the York Hussars. The following year Hudson managed to be reappointed Lord Mayor for 1838-9 despite this being an infringement of the Municipal Reform Act; a third mayorship followed. To mark the coronation of Queen Victoria on June 28, 1838, no expense was spared when he laid on '*an excellent and substantial breakfast*' for the poor and distributed meal tickets for 14,000 of the '*lower orders*', paid for by public subscription.

Hudson was anxious to build a bridge linking the railway station with Lendal and the city centre, promising that the York & North Midland Railway (YNMR) would share the funding with the council. Unfortunately, when the scheme was proposed, the YNMR contribution was conspicuous by its absence. George Leeman, a Liberal, led the outcry, forcing Hudson to contribute to the costs of the bridge design. In 1861 the original bridge, designed by the aptly-named William Dredge, collapsed during construction, with the death of five men. Lendal

Bridge finally opened in 1863, making the ferryman redundant: he received £15 in redundancy money, along with a horse and cart. The toll was used to help pay for the build: half a penny for foot passengers, a penny for animals and two pence for horse-drawn vehicles; the last toll was charged in 1894. The two toll-houses survive as cafes. The new bridge was designed by Thomas Page, who was also responsible for Skeldergate Bridge and Westminster Bridge. The remnants of Dredge's bridge were dredged up from the river and sold to Scarborough Council who used them in the construction of Valley Bridge.

1833 was the year in which Hudson set off on his long roller coaster journey on the railways of England. He attended a meeting at what was then Tomlinson's Hotel in Low Petergate to discuss the construction of the railway line from York to connect with the Leeds to Selby line. Perceptively, he bought 500 shares, making him the largest shareholder. It was at this time that he had the pivotal discussion with George Stephenson to route the London – Newcastle line through York rather than Leeds.

The required Act of Parliament was passed in 1837 with the help of £3,000 in Hudson bribes; this may not have been that difficult to fix as at the time there were 155 MPs in the House who were directors of railway companies. Hudson became chairman of the York & North Midland Railway Company, with George Stephenson as the engineer. He then raised £5,000,000 to link the Midlands with Scotland persuading people to invest by guaranteeing a 6% dividend. Work started on the YNMR line in April 1837 complete with a new station inside the walls in York. The opening of the junction on the Leeds to Selby line took place on 29th May 1839 and at Normanton on 1st July 1840: London was now linked by rail to York. The YNMR leased the Leeds and Selby Railway for £17,000 per year: Hudson lost no time closing the line so that passengers had no choice but to travel on his tracks via Castleford.

From around 1838 the Tories dominated York politics and George Hudson dominated the Tories. As was later to become evident, Hudson lacked the moral rectitude which characterised his opponent, the Quaker Joseph Rowntree. There was that major altercation between the two men during the cholera outbreak of 1832. Another significant conflict was over the appointment of a master at Haughton's School in St Crux. Rowntree got his way and, harbouring suspicions over Hudson's integrity, he went on repeatedly to question in public Hudson's budgets and costings for new projects, and voting irregularities in the mayoral elections.

On Hudson's humiliating fall from power in 1849 Rowntree reluctantly accepted a directorship of the York and North Midland Railway Company which entailed straightening out the books left by Hudson. This he did with his usual rigour and thoroughness, although he may have been motivated by his and other members of his family's substantial investments in the company.

With breathtaking speed a whole raft of other northern lines were opened or brought into Hudson's control around this time. In July 1844 Pickering and Scarborough was approved; in June 1845 the Whitby – Pickering Railway was bought by the YNMR; York to Pickering opened in July 1845 affording a through route from York to Whitby where Hudson owned property. York to Scarborough, which Hudson regarded as potentially the "Brighton of the north", opened on that same day despite objections regarding the company accounts from Joseph Rowntree. On July 1st, 1845 the YNMR took out a lease on the Hull and Selby Railway and in October became joint lessee of the Manchester, Sheffield and Lincoln railway. In 1846 lines from Seamer to Filey and Hull to Bridlington were completed; the following year the line between Filey and Bridlington opened. The YNMR line to Harrogate opened between Church Fenton and Spofforth as did the line from York to Market Weighton. On 8th May 1848 Hull Paragon Station opened and the line from Spofforth to Harrogate was completed. The Selby and Market Weighton link was opened with the line to Beverley following some years later. A direct line to Leeds was on the cards but abandoned after Hudson's demise in 1849. Visible evidence remains at the redundant railway viaduct at Tadcaster.

Hudson as Don Juan.

We have Hudson to thank for championing the introduction of the Railway Clearing House in 1842. It was standard practice for passengers travelling on a journey covering the lines of more than one railway company to have to disembark, change trains and buy a new ticket when they got to the border, as it were. The RCH put an end to this tiresome and tedious requirement by sweeping away all this chopping and changing and establishing a means by which receipts for such journeys could be apportioned fairly depending on the mileage covered on the different rail company lines.

Railroad building requires labourers: Hudson's workforce was made up largely of Catholic Irishmen who were able to come to England by the Catholic Emancipation Act of 1829, settling in York in the Walmgate and Bedern areas.

Hudson's timing was perfect. England was gripped by railway fever, and Hudson was the star of the show. He became chairman of the amalgamated NMR, the Midland Counties Railway and the Birmingham and Derby Junction Railway, to be known as the Midland Railway, which then leased the Bristol and Gloucester Railway and the Birmingham and Gloucester Railway. He sat on the board of the company formed to build a line from Manchester through Buxton and Matlock to north of Derby on the Midland line. 1845 saw the Midland lease the Erewash Valley line and buy the Sheffield and Rotherham Railway. The Midland line from Nottingham to Lincoln opened while the Midland swallowed up the Leicester and Swannington Railway. In 1843 a group of local businessman had formed the Leeds and Bradford Railway company, with Hudson as chairman. This led to a line from Leeds to Bradford via Shipley, as well as a link to the North Midland Railway's terminus at Hunslet Lane, to give connections to the south. The railway opened on 1st July 1846 and was immediately leased by the Midland Railway at the usual favourable terms.

Looking north from York, by 1841 the Newcastle and Darlington Junction Railway was formed with Hudson as chairman; this eventually became the York, Newcastle and Berwick Railway (YNBR). In 1844 a high-level bridge across the Tyne was approved and the line opened as far north as Gateshead. Hudson opened the Richmond branch in 1846; he took over the Hartlepool Dock & Railway which shipped coal from Durham mines to the docks at Hartlepool; he also leased the Clarence Railway which had a similar function serving the Tees. The Durham and Sunderland Railway was absorbed in 1847. Later that

The end of the line for Hudson: the wreck of 'The Royal George' in 1849.

THE GREAT RAILWAY GUY FOR 1849.

The Great Railway Guy for 1949. No coincidence that Guy Fawkes was born, christened and educated (at St Peter's) in York.

year the first section of the Newcastle and Berwick line opened as far as Tweedmouth on 1st July. Hudson leased the Newcastle to Carlisle line and the Maryport & Carlisle Railway.

Hudson companies now controlled 1,450 of the 5,000 miles of track in England; he was in charge of the Midland, the York and North Midland, the York, Newcastle and Berwick, and the Eastern Counties companies– he was indisputably the Railway King. It was revealed in 1845 that he had £319,835 invested in railway shares. He purchased a controlling interest in the Newcastle & North Shields Railway and the Great North of England Railway. His empire now stretched from Bristol to Berwick. It seems that a number of his transactions were not entered in the company's account ledgers. Indicators of his prodigious wealth came in the form of the 12,000-acre Londesborough Estate for which he paid £475,000 to the Duke of Devonshire, and Newby Park in Yorkshire which he bought from Earl de Grey.

But Hudson did not have it all his own way. Arch rival Edmund Denison MP (Sir Edmund Beckett), chairman of the Great Northern Railway, set up the London and York Railway to create a faster link from London to York via Doncaster. Hudson and the Midland Railway opposed the GNR, bizarrely submitting somewhat desperate, impractical plans to build an alternative route through Cambridgeshire and Lincolnshire. Common sense prevailed and the GNR abandoned their plans for a new line and settled for running rights over the other two lines in order that their services could reach York. The earliest services between York and London ran via Doncaster, Retford, Lincoln and Boston; the line through Grantham and Peterborough only opened in 1852.

An ill-judged move in 1845 saw Hudson appointed chairman of the ailing Eastern Counties Railway; he saw this as a way of influencing his alternative York to London route and, despite the line's dreadful chronic punctuality and safety record, Hudson authorised a generous dividend for the shareholders. Relations between him and his vice chairman, David Waddington, whose role it was to falsify the traffic accounts to make returns appear legally earned, deteriorated when Waddington skimmed off £8,000 of ECR money into a Parliamentary slush fund.

Business and politics came in equal measure to George Hudson. In 1846 he shunted through 32 Parliamentary Bills for railway projects costing some £10 million. The same year he emerged from the political sidings to achieve what he considered as the pinnacle of his life: he was elected Tory MP for Sunderland at the 1845 General Election largely won on the promise to bail out the failing Monkwearmouth Dock and the Durham and Sunderland Railway. Hudson companies now controlled over 25% of the railways in England. He also enjoyed part ownership of *The Yorkshire Gazette*, *The Sunderland Times* and *The Railway Chronicle*. When Hudson became an MP he bought a property in Albert Gate in Knightsbridge. Today it is home, no less, to the French embassy. At the other end of the social spectrum, there is evidence that he had a family turned out of their home onto the snowy streets of Sunderland for being a fortnight in arrears with their rent.

Hudson backed the Tory John Lowther at the 1832 general election and again at the by-election the following year. Lowther was finally elected in the 1835 general election. Hudson naively paid into the hands of his enemies when he openly sent the poorer voters who had voted for Lowther a gold sovereign through the post. A Parliamentary select committee investigated but took no further action.

Over the years George Hudson forged a friendship and business relationship with George Stephenson. They became partners opening coalmines, ironworks and limestone quarries around the Chesterfield area; Stephenson agreed to join the board of the York & North Midlands line in 1840. It was not long, however, before Stephenson had doubts about Hudson's integrity and resigned. Here is the text of one of Stephenson's letters to Michael Longbridge, dated 22nd November, 1845:

> 'Hudson has become too great a man for me now. I am not at all satisfied at the way the Newcastle and Berwick line has been carried on and I do not intend to take any more active part in it. I have made Hudson a rich man but he will very soon care for nobody except he can get money by them. I make these observations in confidence to you'.

Hudson was also a friend of the Duke of Wellington. The King of the Iron Road advised the Iron Duke on when best to buy and sell railway shares and, in doing so, made him a good deal of money. In return, ex Prime Minister Wellington visited Hudson's daughter at her private Hampstead school to allay the bullying she was suffering over her father's humble background and her Yorkshire accent. Flowers, and an outing to tea seem to have raised considerably the stock of the young Miss Hudson among fellow pupils and staff.

Two portraits of Hudson – him standing hangs in the Monkwearmouth Railway Station Museum; it is a lithograph by George Raphael Ward, based on an original painting by Sir Francis Grant RA for the Wear Commissioners Office in Sunderland. Him seated is by I Andrews, 1845.

A cartoon showing Hudson fawning to Queen Victoria from *The Illustrated London News* in 1847.

Meanwhile, on the surface, all seemed well in Hudson's kingdom; in January 1846 *The Standard* newspaper published this eulogy:

> Two hundred thousand well paid labourers, representing as heads of families, nearly one million men, women and children, all feast through the bold enterprise of one man. Let us hear what man or class of man ever before did so much for the population of a country.

But *Punch* was on his case after a railway accident at Romford in 1846, allegedly due to savage cost cutting:

> by reason of the misconduct, negligence and insobriety of drivers and sundry stokers, engineers, policemen, and others, your Majesty's subjects, various and several collisions, explosions and oversettings are continually taking place on the railways, your Majesty's dominion.

Hudson's lines were augmented in 1845 with the route to Scarborough; in 1847 Market Weighton and Knaresborough opened, the latter delayed when the first viaduct there spectacularly collapsed into the River Nidd. Later, in 1871, the line from York to Doncaster via Selby shaved miles off the York to London route which hitherto went through Knottingley.

Surreptitiously, George Hudson was making use of inside information and insider dealing to manipulate share prices – profiting handsomely. In 1847 the financial irregularities which would eventually lead to his demise started to emerge. Hudson's railway bubble had burst. In 1848 a damning pamphlet entitled *The Bubble of the Age or The Fallacy of Railway Investment, Railway Accounts and Railway Dividends* alleged that the dividend paid by Hudson's companies were paid out of capital rather than revenue.

Hudson was not above currying favour with royalty. When Prince Albert was elected Chancellor of the University of Cambridge, Hudson provided a royal train to convey Albert and Queen Victoria from Tottenham Station to the city of Cambridge 'in a style of unsurpassed magnificence'. Sycophancy too was 'unsurpassed' as Hudson bowed and scraped before the royal couple.

To make matters much worse, Hudson had been borrowing money at a ridiculously high rate of interest in order to keep some of his vulnerable companies afloat. A payment of

£400,000 was due in 1849. In York the City Corporation led by the indefatigable George Leeman, were demanding payment for the Lendal Bridge project; many of Hudson's allies lost their seats in local elections that year.

Shares prices tumbled and a long-awaited backlash began with undisguised relish. Many who had invested heavily in railway shares were ruined. Hudson had hit the buffers: he resigned from many of his company directorships and had to repay large sums of money which had allegedly been misappropriated. In 1849 he was expelled from York City Council, and, ignominiously, his effigy at Madame Tussauds was reduced to a puddle of melted wax.

The Times summed up the ugly mood one morning in 1848:

> 'It was a system without rules, without order, without even a definite morality. Mr. Hudson, having a faculty for amalgamation, and being so successful, found himself in the enjoyment of a great railway despotism, in which he had to do everything out of his own head and among lesser problems to discover the ethics of railway speculation and management'.

His co-accused brother-in-law Richard Nicholson, took his own life by drowning. A committee of investigation set up by the York, Newcastle and Berwick Company looked closely into Hudson's railway companies; it soon confirmed that he had been falsifying accounts and had concealed the truth about their real financial state. In addition, it revealed that Hudson had been bribing MPs for votes. Hudson had also sold shares to York, Newcastle & Berwick Railway at extortionate prices, to his personal gain, and had sold land to them that was not his to sell. A further committee of inquiry was set up to investigate. Two more followed: one under William Cash for Eastern Counties Railway and another by Midland Railway shareholders. Hudson resigned from both. In spring 1849 the Prance report (YNMR) exposed the valuation of the shares and Hudson was forced to repay £30,000. MP Francis Charteris alleged possible bribery of MPs and another inquiry was instigated. Hudson resigned from the YNMR to avoid being sacked while a committee was set up to look how he had allegedly used YNMR money to build a private station at his pile at Londesborough Park on the Market Weighton line. Throughout 1849 more dirt was unearthed and Hudson was asked to repay £750,000. He sold Londesborough Park, paying £200,000 to the YNBR whose chairman was now George Leeman, to avoid being taken to court.

In 1852 a conciliatory YNMR offered to allow Hudson to settle his outstanding liabilities to them for £50,000; he arrogantly rejected this, leaving the YNMR directors no option but to sue in three separate cases. This was the killer blow, Hudson lost all three cases and had

6. QUEEN VICTORIA & PRINCE ALBERT MEET GEORGE HUDSON, THE RAILWAY KING
Pageant of York 1971

A scene from the 1971 York pageant in which a shrewd and wily George Hudson meets a somewhat uninterested Queen Victoria and Prince Albert at Cambridge University having been conveyed there by a specially built Hudson royal train; little did they know what was to come.

to negotiate a settlement of £72,670 to clear all his debts. Newby Park was sold to Viscount Downe who rubbed salt in Hudson's wounds by engaging George Leeman to do the conveyancing. By the following year the outstanding YNMR debt stood at £16,000; it was taken over by the North Eastern Railway when they merged in 1864.

Despite his serial corruption, Hudson was able to remain as MP for Sunderland until 1859 enjoying the Parliamentary protection this gave him. In the 1852 election he retained his seat with a majority of fifty-four, largely because in 1850 he had secured the opening of a new dock in Sunderland; ironically, his election campaign featured support for a corrupt practices bill. In the 1857 election he was elected again with a further reduced majority. As the Sunderland Dock company declined, so did Hudson's popularity locally and he was defeated at the 1859 election where he polled a meagre 790 out of 4,000 votes. Hudson had lost his Parliamentary immunity from arrest and possible imprisonment.

Despite having agreed to pay everything back, Hudson fled the country, and his creditors. He settled in Boulogne, audaciously returning to England in 1865 for his brother Charles' funeral, and to fight the a seat at Whitby in the general election that year. Harry Thompson was the sitting Liberal MP – chairman of the North Eastern Railway but widely unpopular because he failed to link Whitby to the national rail network and sat back while rival Scarborough became the premier seaside resort on the north east coast. However, before a vote was cast, Hudson was arrested by the Sheriff of York and imprisoned there from July 1865 to October 1866. He was eventually released when the debt for which he was incarcerated was paid off by Tory MP Sir George Elliot, the Atlantic cable pioneer. Elliot and fellow MP Hugh Taylor set up a subscription fund which they launched with a donation of 100 guineas each. It was converted into a trust fund, protected from Hudson's creditors, and provided Hudson with a yearly income of £600. He then moved to Pimlico in London with his wife to live quietly in virtual anonymity.

George Leeman satirized in an 1872 edition of *Vanity Fair*, with top hat.

Hudson fell ill in York in December 1871; he returned to London where he died at home. Ironically, his coffin was taken by train back to York from where he was conveyed and buried at Scrayingham, near to his birthplace. His estate was worth less than £200.

Corruption notwithstanding, George Hudson had nevertheless established York as a major railway centre. His lasting legacy was the formation of the North Eastern Railway Company in 1854, headed by Hudson's enemy George Leeman; York to London could now be done in five hours. Ethical and principled Hudson was not, but he was visionary and made an invaluable and unrivalled contribution to the railways of England. In 1849, in a lame attempt to erase him from local history, George Hudson Street in York was renamed Railway Street; in 1971 the street was renamed again after the Railway King who had presciently brought the railways to York. The old Adelphi pub on the corner of Micklegate took the name 'The Railway King' and a plaque decorates the walls of his former homes at 44 Monkgate and 1 College Street. Ironically, and sadly, George Hudson Street shares with Leeman Road, the distinction of being one of York's shabbiest streets. His name also lives on at Hudson House, formerly the 1968 offices for the north eastern region of British Rail.

It seems that York has always agonised over Hudson, finding it difficult to reconcile his arrant corruption with the priceless and lasting contribution he made to the city. In 1845 *The Yorkshire Gazette* neatly summed up the adulation in which he was held:

> Why is old York like New York? Because in both 'The Hudson' facilitates commercial communication, and has established power and wealth.

In 1849 William Etty, no stranger to controversy and malicious criticism himself, spoke of Hudson's '*honour and honesty…a man I am proud to call my friend*'. *The York and County* appealed for Hudson's rehabilitation in 1968 when it called 'Hudson come back, all is forgiven', echoed in the 1969-1970 *York Civic Trust Annual Report*:

> There is no doubt that George Hudson brought to the City a lasting and important place in the life of the railways of this country…we should make an end to his disgrace.

The obituaries, naturally, came thick and fast. The *York Herald* focused on his 'singular mixture of shrewdness and simplicity',his lack of pretentiousness; The *Yorkshire Gazette* on his tireless charity work and generosity towards the needy and disadvantaged; for *The Sunderland Times* Hudson was 'practically a revolutionist. His name will forever be associated with a gigantic movement which is fast changing the physical, social and moral face of the world...going far to annihilate distance'; to *The Yorkshire Post* Hudson was not alone in his culpability and it was only unshakable fidelity to his friends that saved them from exposure.

Memories, of course, are short and the passage of time can act as a purging filter on the real facts. Vital as his legacy is, visionary that he was, the fact remains that Hudson was a charlatan and a cheat. However, his treatment over the years by the city of his birth is at best shabby, at worst, ignorant. His contribution to York is inestimable and while Guy Fawkes and Dick Turpin have achieved cult status, Hudson, like Joseph's Terry and Rowntree, those other huge York benefactors, remains visually obscure and something of a civic embarrassment. Where are the monuments to all three? Although he robbed many, Hudson neither killed, nor plotted to kill anyone as did Fawkes and Turpin. Perhaps it is best to let *The Times* have the last word, in this extract from its obituary of Hudson on December 16th 1871:

> The first tide in his affairs led on to fortune, but he was afterwards stranded, and neither he nor his schemes could float. A quarter of a century ago he turned all he touched to gold; in after years his name was enough to wither the prospectus in which it was printed. The world which blindly trusted him, which cringed to him and flattered him, avenged itself by excessive and savage reprobation.

George Leeman was a constant thorn in Hudson's side. Born in York in 1809 he was initially articled to Robert Henry Anderson's legal firm and had established a successful legal practice of his own in the city by 1835, Leeman & Wilkinson of York and Beverley. He was alderman for 28 years and was Lord Mayor three times in 1853, 1860 and 1870; he represented York as a Liberal MP between in 1865–8 and 1871–80. Leeman, like Etty and Evelyn, was a tireless defender of York's special and precious antiquities in the face of civic vandalism and promoted the restoration of the city walls.

Leeman had a more long-term view on the scourge that was cholera than that shown by Hudson's solicitudes described above. Leeman went so far as to make York a healthier and safer place to live when he crucially installed the first sewage system with piped clean water since the Romans left. Further afield he was a co-owner of the Rosedale and Ferryhill Iron Company from 1860 to 1877, supplying the Teesside iron and steel works. He was a director of the *York Herald*, chairman of the Yorkshire Banking Company from 1867 to 1880 and chairman of the Railway Association of Great Britain.

George Leeman standing sentinel today near to the railway station. The statue was carved by York sculptor GW Milburn and paid for by public subscription.

Leeman was a participant in the investigations into Hudson's illegal share dealings. In 1849 he succeeded Hudson as chairman of the York, Newcastle and Berwick Railway and was prominent in the establishment of the North Eastern Railway Company in 1854, headquartered in York, one of the wealthiest and most powerful railway companies in the land; he was chairman from 1874 to 1880. Leeman resigned in 1880 after the failure of his mining company; this damaged both his wealth and his health but he remained a member of the board until his death in 1882. His fine, life-size marble statue unveiled in 1885 stands proudly looking towards today's station entrance in York, not far from the Tanner Row station site. The £20,000 it cost was paid for by public subscription. Sadly for Leeman, he is often mistaken for Hudson. He was, after all, a bit of an afterthought: the plinth from which he holds forth was originally earmarked for Hudson. Nevertheless, Leeman has given his name to scruffy Leeman Road which snakes around the present day station and is home to the National Railway Museum; it was originally called Thief Lane, extending into Bishops Fields.

THE IMPACT ON TRADE, INDUSTRY, CULTURE AND TOURISM

The railways brought tourists and other visitors with thirteen trains a day dropping off up to a biblical 341,000 passengers, replacing the two stage coaches which had brought in a mere 23,000 a year. The London – York stage coach route was one of the earliest; this is how it was advertised back in 1698:

> Whoever is desirous of going between London and York or York and London, Let them Repair to the Black Swan in Holboorn, or the Black Swan in Coney Street, York, where they will be conveyed in a Stage Coach (If God permits), which starts every Thursday at Five in the morning.

The London to York coach still took four days for the journey until the mid-18th century – no perceptible improvement in 100 years – an uncomfortable, tiring and often dangerous four days at that. Turnpikes and a new coach, the 'flying machine', led to a reduction in the 1760s and 70s. More journey time was shaved off on the introduction of the mail coach which John Palmer succeeded in getting to pass through York en route to Edinburgh – the 'great North Mail'. The London to York coach journey was further

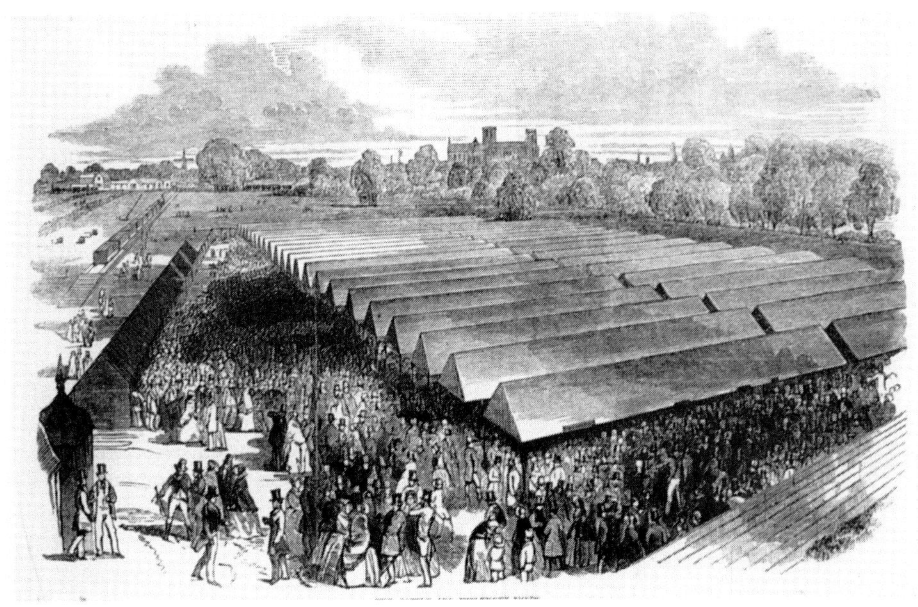

The joint Great Yorkshire and Royal Shows in 1848 on Bootham Stray with one of the branch lines bringing in the visitors at the top left.

York Station from the south with the Minster in the background.

65874 from Dringhouses to Foss Islands goods depot passing Rowntrees on April 10th 1961.

69016 at York.

61813 passing Holgate Station and Holgate Bridge.

shortened in the early 19th century when new methods of road construction methods pioneered by Telford and McAdam were introduced. York had enough mail coaching inns: they included the York Tavern (St. Helen's Square), and the Black Swan (Coney Street), Etteridge's Hotel (Lendal), the White Horse (Coppergate), the White Swan (Pavement), the Elephant and Castle (Skeldergate), the Commercial (Nessgate), the Robin Hood (Castlegate), the Pack Horse (Micklegate), the Old Sand Hill (Colliergate), and the Golden Lion (near Monk Bar).

The railways were, of course, to change everything. The first train service of 1840 slashed six hours off the journey marking the demise of the London to Edinburgh mail coach in 1842. Local services survived for a while: thirteen still ran in 1846, four in 1851, and one in 1867. In 1840 the rail journey from York to London took fourteen hours, reduced to ten hours 20 minutes in 1841 and to six hours ten minutes in 1848. Crowds of people heading for York races would all have taken advantage of the trains to reach the city. By 1841 tourists were arriving from all over the country; theatregoers came from miles around to the Theatre Royal; two Fine Art and Industrial exhibitions in 1860 and 1879, at York Art Gallery, attracted a phenomenal 870,000 people.

Before Harrogate was established as the regular venue for the Great Yorkshire Show, the Royal Agricultural Society and the Yorkshire Agriculture Society held it in different Yorkshire towns, for example, Beverley, Richmond, Doncaster and Leeds, and, for the third time, York in 1848. Attendances regularly exceeded 10,000; the four day 1848 joint Great Yorkshire and Royal Show was something of an extravaganza, visited by Prince Albert. It was held on the extensive 180 acre Bootham Stray and, in an act of railway ingenuity, was served by branch lines from the nearby York to Scarborough railway; one of the first uses of the railways as a major event transport facility. By 1865 York had two postal deliveries a day; a letter posted in London before midday was delivered in York the same evening. The post office in Lendal opened in 1884.

But it was the industries enumerated above who were the main beneficiaries of the railways, for the all-important shipment of imports and exports and the delivery of raw materials and parts. New markets opened up all over the UK, indeed the world. By 1888 there were 294 trains arriving at York every day. The railways made commercial life a lot easier and more cost-efficient for York's industries yet they did not change things significantly – the anticipated influx of new industries or significant expansion of existing industry failed to materialise.

Nevertheless, the railway itself rapidly became the biggest industry in York, the biggest industry York had ever known. The number of people employed in York on the

Asbestos Cement Sheets & Tiles
Bricks, Red & Blue
Cement
Ciment Fondu
Chimney Pots
Celotex Board
Damp Course
Floor Tiles and Quarries
Granite
Hair, Plasterers'
Laths
Lead, Sheet & Pipe
Lime, Warmsworth
Mantels, Wood, etc.
Plaster & Murite
Pudlo
Ranges & Grates
Ruberoid Roofing
Sand & Gravel
Sanitary Pipes
Slag, Sinks
Tiles, Glazed & Roof
Wallboard
Wallties
Whinstone

J. H. WALKER & Co. (York) Ltd. *Tel. No. 2051*

WHOLESALE BUILDERS' MERCHANTS

Gravel Pits : Sand Hutton and Dunnington. *Private Sidings : Foss Islands, L.N.E.R.*

LAYERTHORPE BRIDGE - - YORK

The Foss still in use in the 1920s as an important means of transportation, as this 1928 advertisement for J.W.Walker. builders'merchants shows. They also had the advantage of private sidings courtesy of the LNER.

railways increased from 41 in 1841 to 513 in 1851 of whom 390 immigrated for the work from other towns in the United Kingdom. Many of these were involved in engine repair and building at the railway works where there was a 1200 strong workforce by 1855. Carriage and wagon building followed; this all moved from Queen Street to a site at Holgate and became York's first large scale industry and its biggest employer. By the end of the century there were 5,500 railway workers in the city, nearly 2,000 of whom were skilled. *A History of the County of York: the City of York* tells us that there were three distinct types of railway employment: there were the 'footplate' men, guards, labourers, porters, and station officials who settled in the city; there were administrative office and hotel staff; and there were those employed in the railway works. The works were opened in 1842 with a workshop for engine repairs. From an economic point of view, in 1849 the average value of repairs to engines was a lucrative £15,000 a year; more business came when York started painting carriages. The 1854 amalgamation of railway companies allowed York to expand from repairing to building locomotives and tenders. Despite in 1885 some engine repair work being transferred to Darlington, the number of engines built at York actually increased in what was the busiest period for the engine workshops. After 1900, the company concentrated engine-building and repairs in County Durham, necessitating the closure of the York works in 1905.

All was by no means lost: the wagon and carriage works had meanwhile become more important than the locomotive works. Both had been located in Queen Street until the 1880s when the North Eastern Railway made the decision to concentrate more carriage building in York. New works were therefore built in 1880-1 in Holgate; by 1910 they covered an area of 45 acres. The wagon works had been extended in 1864 facilitating the production of up to 100 wagons weekly, with a further extension in 1875 to eventually cover an area of sixteen acres.

Railway traffic grew inexorably during the later 19th century: in 1863 341,000 passengers were travelling annually to London alone with 58 trains coming into and fifty-five leaving York Station every day. By 1898 an average of 3,200 passengers used the station every day during the summer and 1,650 in the winter; seven rail companies were running services in and out of York. There were real economic benefits to the city: York became a popular place to stop overnight *en route* to London or Scotland, as manifested in the publication of large number of guide books to the city published during the 1850s. The 'city break' was born. The stage coach, however, was doomed, although services were maintained from York to places not on the railway network. York to Leeds took three hours by coach in 1836, in 1841 the journey time by rail was slashed to under an hour; the rail fare was also cheaper.

The Ouse Navigation was also affected, not surprisingly because it was controlled by a corporation which had serious interests in the York and North Midland Railway, interests which might account for the abandonment in 1859 of most of the Foss Navigation bought by the corporation in 1853. But it was not quite that simple, and river traffic held up. Initially there was a steep decline in river coal traffic: an average of 873 coal carrying vessels arrived each year in York between 1830 and 1838, falling to 203 by 1844, the nadir. By 1850, 528 vessels were coming up the river yearly '*due to the recent alterations made by the York and North Midland Railway by which the coal traffic on the river Ouse has been considerably augmented*' [York Corp. Rec., Min. Bk. 14 Feb. 1887]. This can be accounted for by the coal trade that emerged in 1844 from the railway's coal staith in York to London.

Between 1888 and 1889 the millers, Leetham & Sons, agreed with the corporation that they would erect a large mill and silo and pay £200 a year in lieu of dues on the Foss and £600 in lieu of those on the Ouse. By 1900 traffic on the Ouse rose quickly, due mainly to the tonnage carried by Leetham's, but other traffic was also increasing until 1902–3.

Despite all the benefits, however, associated with the emergence of rail transport there was little real change in the overall economic complexion of the city. The price of coal fell, prompting many to believe that this would galvanise an influx of heavy industry.

Tanner Row Station, York's second, with the Rowntree factory and offices on the far right of the picture.

The entrance to the Board of Trade during the 'railway mania' in 1845

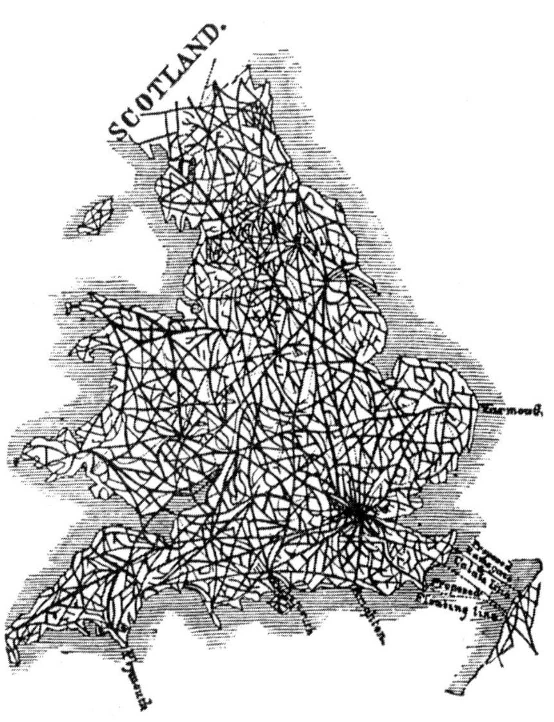

Two cartoons satirizing the railway mania of the mid 1800s both from *Punch*. The caption for the 1845 juggernaut reads 'railway speculation had attained such a hold upon the public mind that thousands rushed madly to their run'.

During the 1830s when coal came laboriously to York via the Aire & Calder Navigation and the River Ouse, it had been between 8s. and 10s. a ton; in the 1840s it hovered between 6s. and 9s.; in 1844 it was 6s. Nine years after cheap coal arrived, railways servicing apart, nothing much had changed in York's industrial economy: the main industries were still flax-dressing and -spinning, comb-making, leather-currying, bone-crushing, glass-making, and glove and mustard-making; chemicals and coffee-roasting. There was no new industry and none of the existing manufacturers expanded rapidly because of the railways. Import and export of materials and finished products was just easier and cheaper, notably for companies like Terry's and iron founders, John Walker. Between 1851 and 1901 the number employed in chemicals, increased from 144 to only 150, in glass manufacture from 159 to 295. In printing no expansion took place until the 1880s: by 1891, 303 were employed compared with 117 in 1871. In iron working numbers rose from 241 to 262 between 1861 and 1891 and then fell back to 185 in 1901. Comb-making more or less disappeared during the 1890s. The leather trades declined from 138 workers in 1851 to 58 in 1891, while linen manufacture became extinct during the 1860s. Flour-milling achieved prominence in the 1860s with Leetham's Mill but in 1891, only 98 persons were returned as working in corn-milling. In confectionery, the extent to which Rowntrees, growth into a major global company was due to the railways is debatable. The potential benefits of rail transport were there for all to see for 40 years without apparently troubling anyone in Haxby Road. They exploited the benefits with their sidings and railway but the firm's explosive growth was surely due to inventiveness and enlightened attitudes on the shop floor, marketing (eventually) and increased wages and disposable income.

The railway industry itself was a different matter. There were 325 employed on the footplate or in railway maintenance and administration in York in 1851, including railway labourers, rising to 671 by 1871 and by 1891 1,548. In 1900 the figure was 2,900.

The rival Midland Railway Settle and Carlisle route to Scotland opened in 1876, encouraging competition and a choice for passengers (which included as well the line offered by the London & North Western Railway Company) in their journeys from London to Scotland and vice versa. Fares came down with the companies anxious to provide the latest in comfort. Four wheeled coaches gave way to six, then rigid eight, bogie eight and then twelve, giving the smoothest ride yet by the 1890s. The Clipper Races did wonders for the delivery of tea from China; the Day Scotch Expresses had a similar beneficial impact on London to Scotland journey times, extending as far north as Aberdeen when the Forth Bridge opened in 1895. York was literally right in the middle of this frenzy. North Eastern could boast in 1902 that the 43 minutes it took to cover the distance from York to Darlington was 'the fastest booked run in the British Empire'.

Leetham's Mill with River Foss transport.

***Below*: Leetham's grain warehouse at Foss Islands with the unusual bridge.**

***Right*: Grain silos at the end of your street – Garden Place in Hungate in the early 1900s. The flour dust and smoke from the coal fuelling the steam engines were decidedly hazardous for residents.**

YORK'S RAILWAY STATIONS

Railways, of course, need railway stations. York has had three. The first was a temporary wooden building on Queen Street outside the walls of the city; this was opened in 1839 by the York and North Midland Railway and owes its fleeting existence solely to the fact that the new arch being built in the city walls and allowing access to the actual proposed station was behind schedule. The temporary building allowed the railway to be officially opened as planned; it was rudimentary to say the least, comprising two rooms – one for the booking clerk, the other for the secretary.

Three years later in 1841 what is known as the Old Railway Station was opened within the city walls, designed by the celebrated York architect GT Andrews and the YNM's engineer Thomas Cabrey. The site was once the home of a Dominican friary and later of the spectacular nursery gardens of James and Thomas Backhouse – known nationally as the Kew of the North. Lady Hewley's Hospital and the 1814 House of Correction were demolished to make way.

Opening day, January 4th 1841, was a public holiday in York with church and Minster bells ringing out and huge crowds celebrating the event. Original plans included a booking office facing Tanner Row (cost £7,900) , a refreshment room, and a train shed. The large shed (300 by 100 feet) was of iron and glass construction supported by cast-iron columns and was unique at the time. The Italianate facade, facing Tanner Row, was 180 feet long; access between the platforms came at the head of the tracks – one of the

The site of the temporary 1839 station pictured in 1939 to mark the centenary. The building on the left is the south end of the 1877 Old Station; that on the right is the No. 1 Erecting Shop of the Locomotive Works. Queen Street bridge is in the background with the city walls behind that.

An engraving of the Old 1841 Station from 1861, from the 1839 GT Andrews archway which was made through the walls. The Scarborough line bays are on the left. The large white building is the station hotel.

The Old Station from the walls in 1926 with smoke billowing from the hotel; each of the rooms had its own coal fire.

Two similar views, one clearly showing the old Station Hotel, the large white building, about 1840.

Looking into the Old Station through one of Andrew's sympathetically built arches *Photo courtesy of YAYAS, part of the superb Evelyn Collection.*

earliest stations in the world with such a facility. The King of Saxony and Charles Dickens were amongst travellers arriving here. The King visited York in 1844 with Carl Gustav Carus, his physician, who left a detailed account of the stay. The entourage travelled 'by steam' from Liverpool to York. Much as he admired the Minster, Carus thought Freiburg and Strasbourg to be even more magnificent.

Andrews was something of a specialist in railway station design with stations at Hull, Huddersfield, Market Weighton and Pocklington already in his portfolio, to name just a few local ones.

The York & North Midland Company (YNM) and the Great North of England Company (GNE) paid for it all but the YNM under George Hudson called the shots with Hudson, also a prominent figure in the corporation, acquiring the substantial corporation property that was required for the site. There was also the vexed question of breaching the city walls for access. After approval was granted by the Yorkshire Philosophical Society, Andrews, York's 'railway architect', was given the job of designing and overseeing the building of the 70 feet high arch with a budget of £1,960.

The station was for passenger traffic only, but the YNM was allowed to use the line for other purposes and to build a goods depot within the walls; the GNE's depot was to be outside although their coal depot was later built on YNM land, and designed by Andrews, who also enlarged North Street Postern to secure better access to the depot. The station opened later with GNE passenger services from Darlington starting on March 30th.

Such a momentous project was always going to have ramifications for the area around Toft Green. Railway Street (later George Hudson Street, then Railway Street again) was laid out between Micklegate and Tanner Row; a new road was built across its land between Tanner Row and Tanner's Moat, and another new road and arch linked up to the GNE coal depot through North Street Postern making distribution to the city and its environs much easier and quicker. The coal depots had a beneficial affect on the price

Coming out of the Old Station with royal train carriages. July 28th 1949. Andrew K. Mc Cosh 60003 is about to take Princess Elizabeth and the Duke of Edinburgh back to London. Among other things McCosh was President, British Iron and Steel Federation, Director, London and North Eastern Railway.

Two views of the Old Station from the walls.

locally: in six years the price plummeted from £16s 6d a ton to £6s 6d. So much for the surface level disruption; below the surface on the site the remains of Roman bath houses were discovered; the railway companies agreed to compensate the workers for any finds which were donated to the Yorkshire Philosophical Society for their museum, later the Yorkshire Museum.

In 1845 a second arch was sensitively introduced through the city wall after the opening of the Scarborough line; three extra platforms were added by 1851 with the train shed extended to cover them by 1861. Despite fervent opposition from other hoteliers and publicans a hotel was then built across the head of the lines to link the two blocks of the station. Andrews was again the architect.

On the down side, the site was restricted preventing much further expansion, although a platform beyond Holgate Bridge was completed in the early 1860s. The station was known as the 'dead-end' because traffic from Newcastle or London and from Scarborough was obliged to come into the station and reverse back out in order to continue the journey. Time consuming and tedious, this was not consistent with the efficiencies and speed associated with the railway age. The use of ticket platforms to hold trains while the engines went round was also dangerous but was allowed to continue. Holgate Bridge with its platforms for 43 coaches was generally used for York races and for other special events. The last use for Knavesmire was on August 24th 1939 when the platforms were known as Holgate Excursion Platforms. Coal depots proliferated upstream between what is now Lendal Bridge and Scarborough Bridge; they were served by four tracks branching off from the GNE line in 1870. There were 42

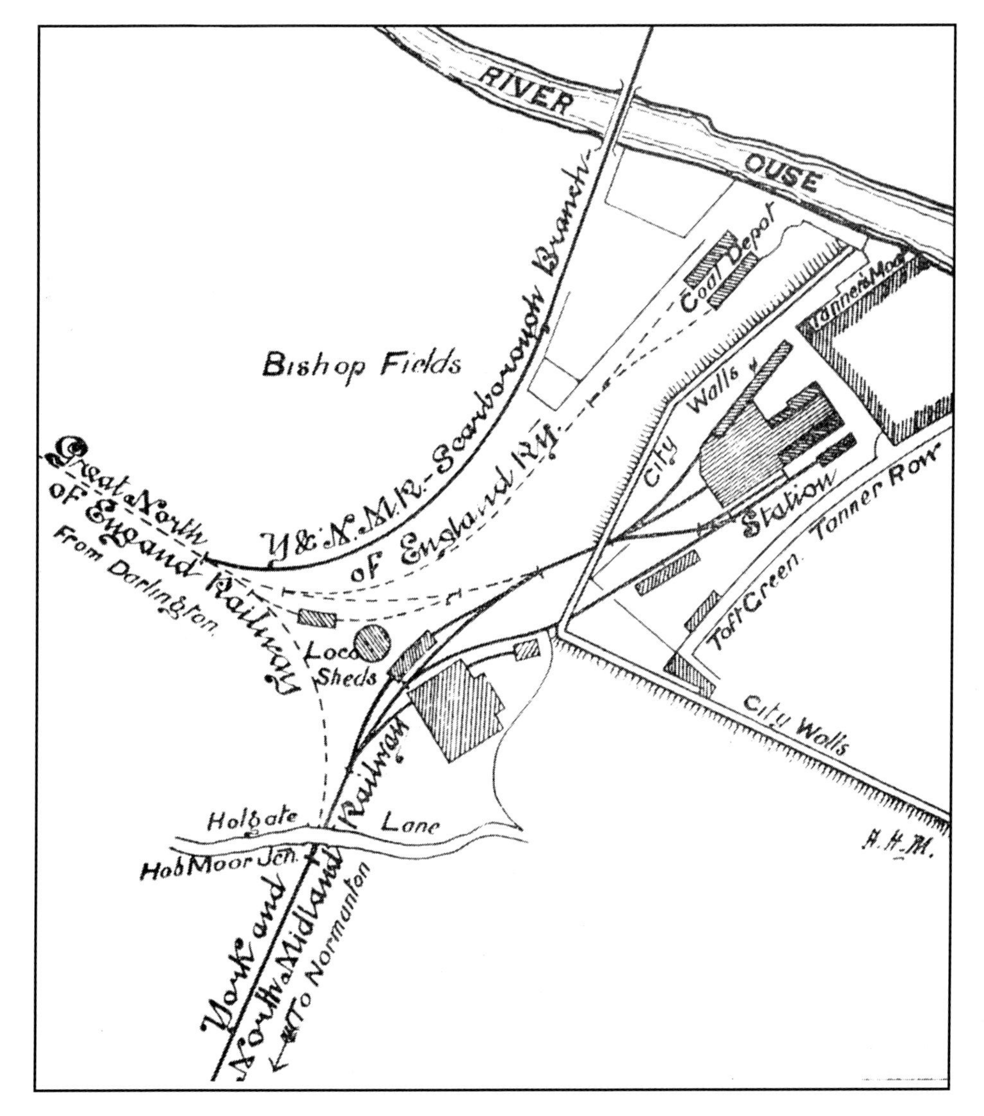

Map of the Old Station originally published in an issue of *The Railway Magazine*, reproduced in the BR *North Eastern Magazine*, April 1963.

Converting the Old Station to smart, eco-friendly council offices.

coal cells and seven lime cells. To satisfy the need for goods facilities a 'merchandise station' (also known as the Sack Warehouse) was built.

In 1850 a cup of tea or coffee in first class cost 8d, 6d in second; breakfast, luncheon or tea in first was 2s, 1s 6d in second.

As noted, the Old Station could not satisfy the needs of York for very long, given the huge expansion of railway services nationwide and the magnet for services that York was becoming. Prodigious amounts of goods and raw materials, hordes of people pursuing business or seeking pleasure, piled on to the railways and York, as a hub, saw a lot of this traffic. Furthermore, there were complaints from the Great Northern and from the Board of Trade inspecting officers regarding the many accidents caused by propelling full passenger trains over long distances in the confines of the cramped station. A report dated as early as September 17th 1845 compiled by the directors of Great Northern Rail Company described the '*inconvenience of the York station*' – no doubt a polite euphemism – and, more bluntly, '*a serious evil*'. The report went on to detail the nature of this pernicious situation:

> 'There is no room to allow of the simultaneous arrival of several trains, the consequence of which is that it is a daily occurrence that trains are kept for a considerable while outside the Walls waiting for a train to be backed out, or otherwise got rid of, before they can be admitted'.

York's magnificent roof – in the early 20th century and 100 years later in 2014.

Scarborough Bridge today, undergoing maintenance.

The Andrews arches today.

Leech's cartoon in *Punch* showing chaos on the platform during a refreshment stop. Note the serialised Dickens' *Little Dorrit* on the news stand.

The ticket office in the 1930s when it was geographical.

Below Clockwise from top left: Four views from the outside over time showing changes in traffic type: very little in the way of city transport or traffic around in 1900, Horse and trap, motor cars on the rank and tram and motor car. The tram is heading for Acomb in the 1920s. It was introduced in 1912 and carried 30 passengers on the upper deck with a further twenty-two on the lower.

Clockwise from top left: seven views of life on the platforms over time, Tails, top hats and hand carts; Joseph Pennell's 1895 depiction of York Station; gas lamps, milk churns, ladies' first class and the pre-bridge subway; John Sampson, bookseller and newsagent outside his shop on the station; the much-needed footbridge, after 1900, the original bookshop was here at the foot of the steps; railway offices and gentleman's lavatory; railway staff, travelling ladies and platform vendors.

The garage and the laundry.

The aim was to ensure that the York route, the York & North Midland route, was always the route of choice to Scotland. This did not help.

In 1865 it was decided to build a new station outside the walls and the necessary Bill went through Parliament. The station would be between the Scarborough line and old Thief Lane: two connecting lines would serve as the 1 ¼ mile main line and the furlong connection to the existing Scarborough branch. Financial issues and falling shares delayed the opening until June 1877. It was designed by three NER architects, Thomas Prosser who retired in 1874, Benjamin Burleigh who died in 1876 and William Peachey. On the opening of the new station, the Old Station was relegated to a train park for rolling stock. From time to time it performed more prestigious roles: the first class refreshment room was used from 1928 to 1966 to house the Small Exhibits collection of the Railway Museum; the Festival of Britain display took place there in 1951; the Inverness – King's Cross sleeper parked there; and the buildings housed the BR medical centre.

At the time the new, third station with its thirteen platforms was the largest in the country; its majestic curved train shed covered the four through traffic lines. The spectacular glazed roof measures 800 by 234 feet supported by imposing iron columns; the widest span covers platforms eight and nine and is 81 feet; it is flanked by two 55 feet spans; 42 feet below, its main platform is 1,692 feet long. It is built of yellow Scarborough brick with Tadcaster stone dressing. The roof owed something to the roof designs at Newcastle and Brunel's Paddington. York Station truly deserves the cynical description as *'a very splendid monument to extravagence'*, or, in an allusion to the Parthenon in Athens, the Propylaeum. It cost £400,000. The present imposing Royal York Hotel was part of the project – designed by Peachey, opening in 1878 and extended in 1882.

Again, changes were made locally. Two more arches punctured the city wall near to where the NER War Memorial is to allow roads to get to the old Thief Lane, which was renamed Station Road , post-Hudson. The continuation of Thief Lane into Bishops Fields was diverted to give access to the new coal and lime depots; after the statue of George Leeman went up in 1885, it was renamed Leeman Road. Scarborough Bridge was rebuilt and a bridge replaced the level crossing in Queen Street.

The first train to leave the new station was the 5.30am on Sunday June 25th , 1877; it was heading for Scarborough across the newly adapted Scarborough Bridge. The two 75 feet spans were replaced with wrought iron and the public footpath running in between the tracks was, prudently, moved to the south east side of the bridge.

Platform fourteen was built – of wood – in 1900 for the Royal Agricultural Show crowds held that year in York. Additional platforms came in around 1909 and between 1938 and 1941. The colour scheme was maroon, mauve and white; lighting was by gas supplied by NER's dedicated gas works near Severus Junction (York Yard North). In 1900 the fine footbridge first spanned the tracks complementing the subway. There were, of course, no dining cars on trains in those days – the first rolled into York in 1893 and even then only in one train in each direction: the main services from King's Cross paused for 20 minutes to allow passengers to grab something to eat and drink from the refreshment rooms constructed on platform eight – a recipe for chaos when trains were running late. A permanent tea room was built on that platform in 1906; it served as the staff canteen during the Second World War.

1936 saw the opening of the 1,180 feet platforms fifteen and sixteen. In 1939 plans were laid to have the station re-signalled with coloured lights and power operated points; the platforms were renumbered: platform nine used to be platform five, for example; and platforms fifteen and sixteen came into service. A new signal box was installed above platforms thirteen and fourteen in 1951 with the eventual introduction of the delayed re-signalling. 1941 saw the change at the ticket office from a geographical system to alphabetical. A-K, Leeds and London were at the three main windows; the others catered for L-Z Leeds and London; and Army, RAF and Navy.

A station as vital as York is to the national rail network does not come just with sheds and platforms alone. The new station brought with it a whole host of ancillary institutions and buildings. Many of these are dealt with in detail later in the book.

The YNM offices were originally in the basement of the York Subscription Library (founded 1794) in St. Leonard's Place, but the GNE financed purpose-built offices over the booking-office block of the old railway station in 1841. Further office space was found when the hotel at the new station was opened and the old hotel and the station itself were converted to offices.

The NER opened a library and reading-room in Queen Street in 1872. But to cater for the 4,000 NER staff they built the Railway Institute in Queen Street which opened in 1889. The Railway Centenary Exhibition was held in York in 1925, the success of which led to the opening of a Railway Museum in 1928, again in Queen Street. A branch of British Transport Historical Records was set up at York in 1955 to facilitate railway related research.

The NER Laundry built its own 6,600 square feet facility in 1894 to service its dirty washing from hotels and refreshment rooms. It was built in Heworth on the Foss Islands

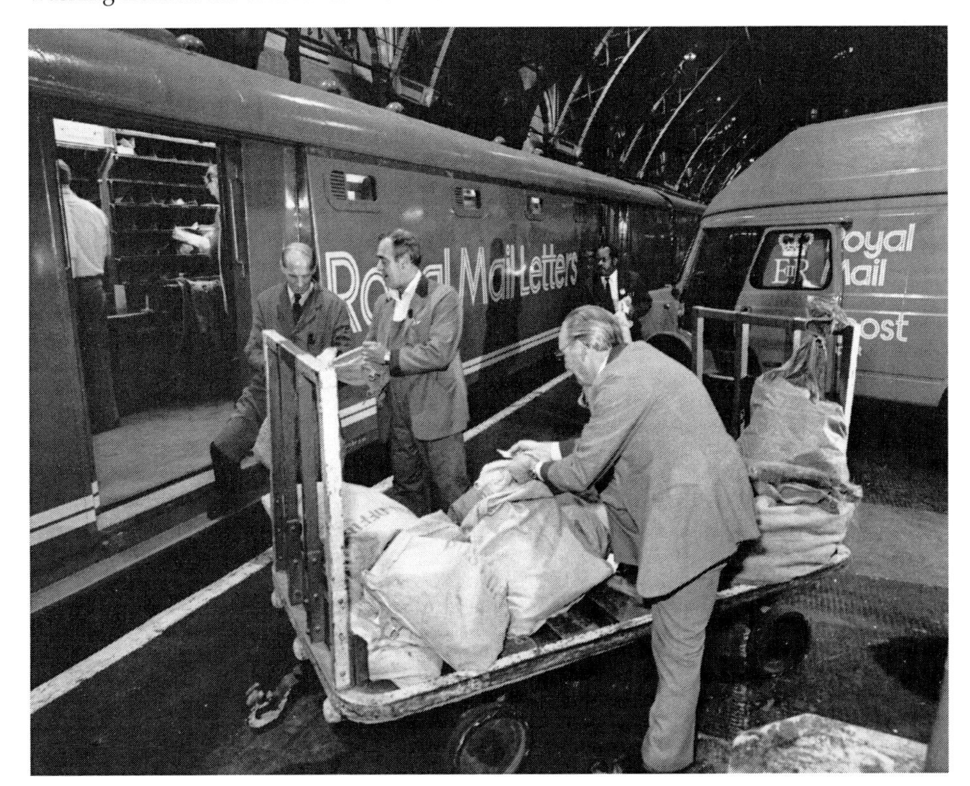

Post office sorting. Photo © *York Press.*

Branch with sidings for the delivery of coal needed for the boilers. Perversely, delivery of laundry from the station was made by road. In 1930 the laundry was more than doubled in size to 14,000 square feet to allow it to handle 4 million items per year.

A carriage washing plant was built in 1930 at Clifton carriage sidings. The eight vertical revolving drums – four on each track – enabled a twelve carriage train to be washed in about twelve minutes.

A garage was built in Leeman Road for guests staying at the then Royal Station Hotel opposite; it was extended by the LNER in 1924. The garage superseded the facilities made available by the NER Road Motor Department at Queen Street. It later became known as Foxton's Garage. The Post Office sorting office next door is joined to the station by a subway which runs under platforms four, five, six and seven; lifts connect it to platform 8B.

Sir Edward Lutyens (he of the Whitehall Cenotaph) was commissioned to design the NER First World War obelisk memorial which stands outside the former NER offices; the budget was £20,000. After much deliberation and controversy the 54 feet high Portland Stone memorial was finally unveiled in June 1924, the inordinate delay caused by the dithering of the York Corporation agonising over the view from the (Lendal) bridge. Six thousand people attended the unveiling. The fifteen feet high screen walls (these had to be reduced in height) bear the names of the 2,236 men who died. The memorial occupies the former site of one of NER's private fire stations and, even earlier, three sidings which stretched down to Lendal Bridge.

The NER War Memorial soon after being unveiled.

The NER goods depot in 1907; the double sided weigh house is the building to the right.

YORK STATION HOTELS

During the days of the stage coach, travellers stayed at coaching inns when they broke or ended their journeys. The emerging railway companies soon realised that this was not the answer to rail travellers' accommodation needs – something very close to the station was required for those who had come to the end of their railway journey or were breaking that journey. And so the station hotel was born. Indeed, the early railway hotels were actually the first travel packages: rail and hotel, city breaks.

The Old Station was complemented by a hotel which was built at the head of the rails; it opened in February 1853 to a design by Andrews. Fittingly, it was originally called The Station Hotel and had fifteen reception rooms and 55 bedrooms. It became known as Scawin's Railway Hotel after Sarah Scawin bought it in 1854 with it bearing her name long after she sold it in 1869; it was demolished in 1900 after the new hotel at the new railway station became well established. Scawin's could boast as one of its guests Queen Victoria who stayed there in September 1854. Her Majesty had stayed in York in September 1849 on her way to open the High Level Bridge at Newcastle; the owners decided that this entitled them to add 'Royal' to the name of the hotel. The manager was a Mr Holliday; charges included what would now be called continental breakfast 1s 6d, or with meat, 2s, the same price as luncheon; dinner was 2s 6d in the coffee room or 3s in a private room; beds were between 1s 6d and 2s 6d, whole 'attendance' was 1s 6d per day; boot cleaning was 6d while a waiter was charged at between 6d and 1s.

Old hotel, Old Station.

The first station hotel at the Old Station in an engraving published by Bock & Co London in 1866.

Scawin's Family Hotel.

When Scawin's closed the hotel was converted into offices. The contents and furnishings were obviously not deemed suitable for the new hotel and were auctioned off. The contents of all the receptions and bedrooms were joined in the eight day sale by 2,200 pieces of silver plate, oil paintings and etchings; it all realised £2,516 9s. If nothing else it gives an impression of the luxury to be had at Scawin's during its lifetime as a hotel.

A sumptuous hotel was part of the plan when the new station was built, although it did not open until 1878. Nothing if not grand and elegant, its five storeys offered 100 stylish bedrooms at fourteen shillings a night. Three entrances allowed access: the town entrance, the garden entrance and the tiled octagonal entrance – used by patrons arriving by train. The garden, or west, entrance, was lost when the 27 west wing extension was built in 1896; this took the name 'Klondyke' as it was the year of the Klondike gold rush in the Yukon. A new garden entrance was built in 1939. The original electric doorbell survives with its panel of buzzers and discs by the porter's desk. The coffee room with its splendid views of the river is now the restaurant while the east wing boasted a smoke-room and a billiard room with magnificent ceramic tiles. The wooden reading racks in what was the oak-paneled reading room in the Klondyke Wing have survived.

Advertising for the Royal York Hotel, one of the North Eastern Railways hotels.

Royal Station Hotel in 1910.

The original lounge.

below left: the lounge today
below right: the beautiful tiles decorating what is now the spa.

YORK'S INDUSTRIAL RAILWAYS

Private railways designed to do the donkey work were almost *de riguer* by the end of the 19th century. Many large industrial concerns used them for transportation of goods and materials: Dorman Long in Middlesbrough, Fry in Bristol, Cadbury in Bournville and Lever in Port Sunlight are just a few examples. York was no exception.

YORK GASWORKS

In 1826 any town with a population exceeding 10,000 was likely to have a gasworks. York was one of the first to get gas when, in 1824, the York Gas Light Company (YGLC) was established between the Foss and Monk Bridge and introduced York to gas lighting, or 'the lamp that wouldn't blow out'. The YGLC enjoyed a monopoly in gas supply until York Union Gas Light Company (YUGLC) set up their works in Hungate. After years of rivalry, with workmen from the former filling in the latter's excavations, they merged in 1847 to form the York United Gas Light Company, later shortened to the York Gas Company, operating at both the Hungate and Monk Bridge sites, in 1850, the Hungate works were closed. Due to restrictions on space at the Old Works at Monk Bridge, a completely new works was built at Heworth Green in 1885 – the New Works.

Before the railways came coal was shipped to the gas works from the York & North Midland Railway staiths on the Ouse, then along the Foss – or through the congested city on carts; as soon as the new site was mooted a rail junction connecting to the NER Foss Islands Branch was constructed allowing for the easier movement of 50,000 tons of coal. The railway opened in 1915 and was in service until 1959 with locomotives operating on an electrified railway – names were *Kenneth* built in 1885 arriving in 1919, and *Centenary* built in 1924; livery was olive green with red, yellow and gold lettering. The power supply came from a direct current of 500 volts along a private line from the Corporation Power Station.

In 1824 there were 250 consumers; this had risen to 34,000 by 1963. In 1912, coverage was extended to seven miles from the Ouse Bridge to take in Haxby, Wigginton and Strensall.

The entrance to the Old Works with an overhead electric tram train passing in the background.

York gasworks showing the rail bridge linking the New and Old Works across the River Foss. Picture published originally in Darsley, *Industrial Railways of York.*

lower right: The Kerr Stuart built in 1912. Picture published originally in Darsley, *Industrial Railways of York.*

lower left: York's electricity generating station about 1905. It is said that the ground round the plant used to shake and vibrate from the noise and the 30,000 horse power.

YORK CORPORATION POWER STATION AND DEPOT

The (electric) lights were first switched on in 1899 when York Corporation Electricity Committee's electricity generating station opened on the Foss. By 1929 there were 16,470 consumers paying 3½d per unit. The number of units sold (in millions) were: domestic 180; public lighting 38; industrial 219.

The chimney survives to this day. Electrical equipment was supplied by Siemens, including the electric tramway locomotive delivered in 1912 – the *Kerr Stuart* 1269. As at the gas works, the function of the railway was to deliver coal, in this case to the boilers. The 180 yards of railway and sidings were completed in 1904. A second locomotive built by Metropolitan Vickers was added in 1942.

LEETHAM'S MILLS

As we have seen, Leetham and Sons were one of the biggest firms not just in York but in the British four-milling industry in the second half of the 19th century. The Hungate flour mill was founded by Henry Leetham in 1860 and extended to the Foss site in 1885. After Castle Mills lock was rebuilt in 1888, Leetham's was one of the chief users of the river, situated as they were between the river and Wormald's Cut, with access by a four storey high level gantry bridge across the Foss to Hungate Mills. By 1900 Leetham's had expanded with operations in Hull, Newcastle and Cardiff; Leetham's was producing 112 sacks per hour by this time.

Initially, around 1900, railway activity was confined to the warehouse on the Foss Islands side of the River Ouse where four horses were used for shunting as NER locomotives were prohibited from crossing Foss Islands Road. In 1904 Leetham's were denied permission to

Leetham's Mill warehouse at Hungate. The nine-storey water tower with battlements and turrets is still a famous York landmark, visible for miles around. Rowntrees bought the warehouse from Spillers in 1937 for cocoa bean storage. Picture published originally in Darsley, *Industrial Railways of York*.

Rowntree train at No 1 Landing Stage in Wigginton Road in 1971.

By 1887 a horse-drawn truck or rulley was needed to take the day's goods from the Tanner's Moat factory to the station each day. This shows Wiliam Laycock doing just that; he joined NER in 1868 and did the trip every day from 1887 until his death in 1911.

deploy steam engines to haul wheat wagons from their sidings due to the un-navigability of the Ouse. In 1919 it seems that this decision was finally reversed and steam haulage began.

Leetham ran three locomotives: *Neptune* (1863), *Tissington* (1893) and one other – although never at the same time. Essentially, bulk grain arrived at the mill in barges and bagged flour and meal left by train after overnight loading. The daily total was twelve to 20 wagons although up to 100 was not unknown. The famous steam paddle tub *Anglia* was owned by Leetham's; this was the vessel which had towed Cleopatra's Needle from Egypt to England and had come to York in 1916 to be converted into a store ship.

ROWNTREE & CO

Rowntree Halt at Hambleton Terrace was a small, unmanned railway stop on the Foss Islands Branch Line on the southern edge of the chocolate factory. The LNER opened it in 1927 to provide an un-timetabled passenger service to the Rowntree factory for workers commuting from the Selby and Doncaster areas. It was not much more than a signal and a single short platform situated a few yards west of the siding that allowed freight directly into the factory complex. There was no extra charge for the leg to the Halt from York Station, either to the commuter or to Rowntree. The Halt was closed in 1988.

Between 1890 and 1895 Rowntree's bought one locomotive, *Marshall* to assist in the construction of the Haxby Road factory, and had one-and-a-half miles of standard gauge track at their disposal. *Marshall* was sold in 1895 and *Newton* was then bought from T.A. Walker who had used it in the building of the Manchester Shipping Canal. It was put into use coal shunting at the factory. Locomotive No.2 was bought new in 1909 sharing general duties with a third locomotive bought in 1915. A fourth, the ramshackle *Swansea*, was bought in 1943 with its distinctive vivid green livery. The other locomotives were brown lined with cream. The company also owned 38 wagons. The company had seven miles of track and a short 18-inch narrow gauge line.

BRITISH SUGAR CORPORATION, POPPLETON

Built in 1926 by the Anglo-Scottish Beet Sugar Corporation had a slicing capacity of 1,000 tons a day. Rail was the method of choice for moving sugar beet until the development of road transport, with the result that much of the Poppleton site was given over to railway sidings. On arrival, wagons were driven over a weighbridge to assess gross weight and a sample was taken to calculate sugar content. Unloading then took place in the beet silo area, either by high pressure water jet (Elfa guns), by mechanical tipping or by pitchfork. Empty wagons were then reweighed to find the actual tonnage of beet delivered.

During the fourteen week season the factory operated around the clock; 15-20,000 wagons passed through the factory in a season. A wagon was turned round every five or six minutes. Poppleton started with four-coupled saddle tanks.

lower left: **Elfa guns washing out sugar beet at Poppleton in the 1930s. Picture published originally in Darsley, *Industrial Railways of York*.**

lower right: **Wagons waiting to be unloaded at Poppleton in 1943.**

THE DERWENT VALLEY LIGHT RAILWAY

There were two additions to the main lines running to and from York. Having bought the Foss Navigation in 1853, the corporation tried to persuade the NER to build a branch line across the Foss Islands district to Walmgate Bar to service the cattle market and industry on the eastern side of the city. The 1¾-mile line was opened in December 1879, running from the YNM's Scarborough line to a goods station near Walmgate Bar.

DVLR was born of the Light Railways Act of 1896. Farmers southeast of York needed a better way of reaching the markets at York and Selby with their produce than the existing rail routes could offer; a number of land owners approached Escrick and Riccall rural district councils to explore the possibility of a light railway. The result – DVLR – ran over sixteen miles from Layerthorpe to Cliffe Common, a small station on the NER line between Selby and Market Weighton. The northern terminus at Layerthorpe linked into the NER's Foss Islands branch, and became DVLR headquarters. It opened for goods and livestock in 1912 and for passengers in 1913 with three week day trains in each direction with an extra service between Layerthorpe and Wheldrake. Scheduled time was 50 to 58 minutes; carriages were first and third class, ex NER painted dark blue with gold lettering. There were eleven stations on the line, from Layerthorpe south to Osbaldwick, Murton Lane, Dunnington Halt, Dunnington (for Kexby), Elvington, Wheldrake, Cottingwith, Thorganby, Skipwith and Cliffe Common. All stations handled goods as well as passenger traffic and all had their own sidings. There was only ever one signal on the line, at Wheldrake, where a sharp bend immediately before the station hid the level crossing from the driver and demanded a warning. The original track was bought second hand from the Midland Railway's Settle Carlisle line.

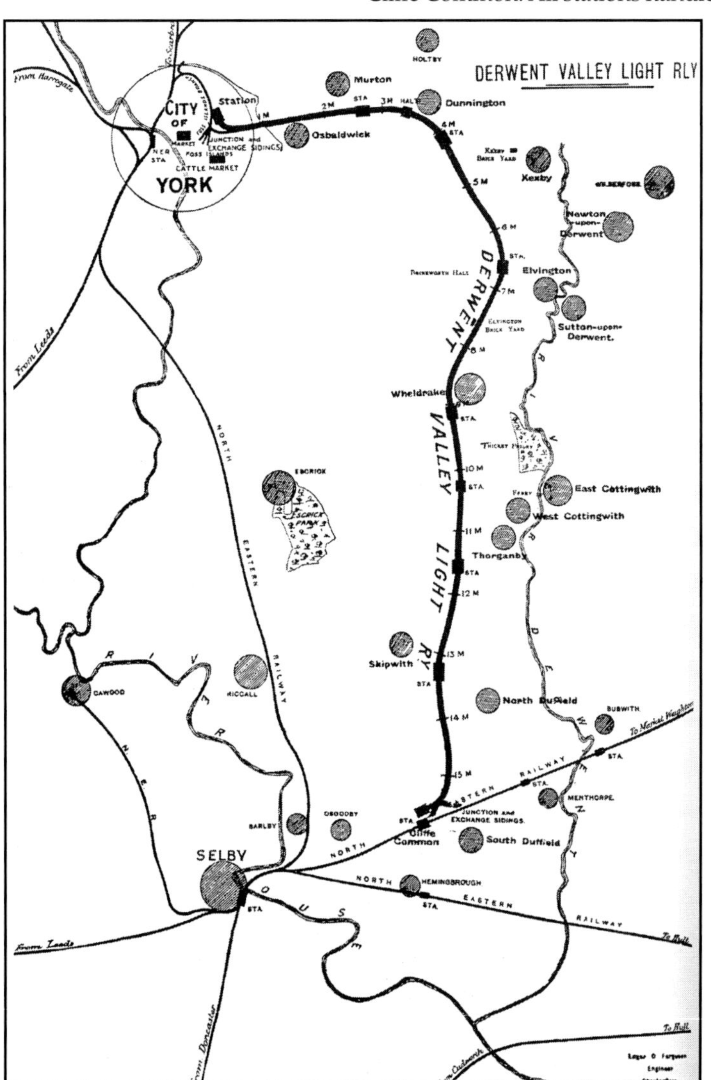

A 1913 map showing the DVLR. *From the RD Pulleyn Collection.*

By 1916 passenger traffic from villages served along the Derwent was declining due to competition from bus services; in the 1920s passenger numbers dropped steeply from 49,000 at the end of the First World War to 18,000 in 1925. Two Ford rail buses were introduced in 1924 coupled back to back but, despite reducing the cost to 5d per mile from 1s, the line was closed for passenger traffic in 1926 although it was still used for healthy goods traffic until 1958.

From the 1930s goods traffic was on the up, expanding from the increasing Dig for Victory farm produce to include chemicals and minerals and benefitting from the restrictions on road transport caused by fuel rationing. During the Second World War the government built an aerodrome at Wheldrake, which became a supply dump for motor spirit, explosives and timber; mustard gas was stored at Cottingwith Station. The line was never picked up by Luftwaffe reconnaissance because of the natural camouflage it obtained from weeds left to grow due to deferred maintenance.

The Derwent Valley Light Railway survived Grouping, and was never nationalised, and so has always been a private railway. The line is also known as the Blackberry Line – from the days when it was used to transport blackberries to markets in Yorkshire and London.

Above: York Layerthorpe.

Left: A hired BR steam locomotive, 65700, at Dunnington Station; the daily freight train.

Two Ford Railcars coupled back to back at Layerthorpe in the 1920s. *Photo by Photomatic.*

PASSENGERS, FREIGHT & SIGNALLING

Passenger services from York is a seemingly endless story from 1839 to the present day. Suffice to say that it marked perpetual and inexorable growth as routes and lines proliferated and the demand from passengers expanded. Here are a few snapshots to give a flavour of the rapidly developing situation.

In 1841 there were York & North Midland trains leaving at 6.30 am, 8.45 am, 11.30 am, 4.00 pm and 6.00 pm for Normanton, Sheffield, Derby, Birmingham, Nottingham and London with connections to Selby, Leeds and Hull from the 11.30am and 6.00pm; Manchester could be reached via the three morning trains. Leeds, Selby and Hull trains left at 8.00 am and 3.00 pm. In 1847 there were five daily services to Scarborough two of which were non-stop taking 55 minutes.

In 1872 there were five Edinburgh to King's Cross trains calling at York with specially-built carriages for the service; the Scarborough trains had increased to eight and the Market Weighton Branch enjoyed four departures to Hull. There were six trains to Harrogate, one of which stopped only at Knaresborough and a service to Gilling and Helmsley. All in all there were 67 trains pulling out of York every 24 hours. Over the next 30 years or so direct services to Aberdeen, Bath, Cardiff, Glasgow and Manchester came on stream. In the summer of 1911 180 trains were leaving York each day.

By 1898 Running Powers Agreements allowed six separate companies to operate through York, making it second only to Carlisle which hosted seven. They were Great Northern Railway (GNR) from 1848; Midland Railway (MR) from 1874; Lancashire & Yorkshire Railway (L&Y) including cattle traffic; Great Eastern Railway (GER) from 1893; from 1893 London & Northwestern Railway (LNWR) and Great Central Railway (GCR) in 1898.

The 1930s were momentous for passenger services. This was when *The Flying Scotsman* was operating at its zenith and the Sir Nigel Gresley streamlined 'streaks' hurtled down the line between Edinburgh and London most famously in the guise of the 'Silver Jubilee' train pulled by such icons as *Silver Link, Silver King* and *Silver Fox*. This was followed by the 'Coronation' service in 1937.

Locally, the halt at Rowntrees linking the factory to the main station opened in 1927 largely for the benefit of commuters from Selby, and for freight through its link to the Foss Islands freight branch. Services to Haxby, Stensall and Flaxton closed for passenger traffic in 1930.

The Newcastle – Bristol express leaving platform 8 published in *The Railway Magazine* Vol 95 No. 583 p. 305: Twenty- Four Hours at York.

60018 Sparrow Hawk pulling out of York in the 1950s. *Photograph by Eric Treacy.*

York cattle market in the 1910s.

Both the YNM and the GNER were quick to set up freight depots in York to compete with the existing horse and cart and river traffic competition. The confectionery industry in the shape of Rowntree, Terry and Craven, Leeman's and the sugar beet plant at Poppleton became major users of rail freight. The Cattle Market (opposite what is now The Barbican Centre) was another significant user with livestock arriving from Ireland for offloading at Foss Islands. In 1923 7,884 wagons of livestock came to York, making it second only to Newcastle in the north east as a livestock depot.

In 1861 the 'Meat Train' left Newcastle at 3.55 am arriving York at 8.30; the 'Aberdeen Express Goods' arrived in York at 2.15 pm having departed Newcastle at 9.30 am. The 'Fish Train' left Newcastle at 3.10 pm and arrived at 7.40 pm in York. A lot of coal came through York, for example on 'Coke for Normanton', 'GN Coal' or 'Cootes train', Cootes being an East Anglian coal merchant.

A railway branch line extending about 1 ¾ miles opened in 1880, connecting the NER York to Scarborough Line to the large industrial area and freight depot in the Foss Islands area of the city. Apart from the Rowntree's factory on Haxby Road, there were sidings used by the York Gas Company at Monk Bridge; the York Corporation power station and refuse destructor; Leetham Mills' Navigation Warehouse at the junction of the River Foss and Wormald's Cut; and the British Transport Hotels laundry. In 1913 The Foss Islands end was connected to the Derwent Valley Light Railway northern terminus at Layerthorpe Station.

York Layerthorpe.

Inside the Loco Yard box.

The 1951 44 feet long train movement panel with signalmen.

Signals on display at the National Railway Museum. ©*York Press.*

Signals looking into the station from Scarborough Bridge with Waterworks Box on the right and platforms 4-7 on the left.

Before 1877 signalling was primitive to say the least with bells and hand signals being used to alert signalmen down the line to expect a train imminently. Needless to say, this resulted in a series of accidents. In the late 1870s old York Station was controlled by a number of signal boxes including Archway (so called because it was close to the new arch in the walls), and, going south, Locomotive Yard Box, South Ticket Platform Box, Middle Box and Holgate Bridge Box – all usefully descriptive of their locations. As the years passed these were upgraded, replaced and added to, or closed according to requirements. The biggest change came in 1937 when it was agreed that colour light signals be installed, extending to Copmanthorpe and Naburn in the south and to Poppleton Junction in the north. The new signals meant a new signal box in York Station. the Second World War delayed the project which was finally completed in 1951.

The box, unobtrusively nestled between platforms thirteen and fourteen north of the footbridge, goes unnoticed by most passengers. In 1951 the 44 feet long illuminated train movement panel inside boasted 867 switches, 5,410 miniature light bulbs for track circuit indications, 317 track circuits; and the facility to set up 827 routes extending over 33 ½ miles of track. At the time it was one of the biggest contracts ever awarded for track signalling and was the largest route relay interlocking system in the world; cost exceeded £562,000. The huge 44 feet panel was manned by four signalmen; these were complemented by a traffic regulator and a fifth signalman who took telephone calls. Routes can be set up with astonishing speed: a route which took up to forty lever movements with the manual system could be completed in ten seconds with the new system.

Propane gas point heaters prevented the signals snagging in snow. The train announcer occupied a glass fronted cubicle overlooking the panel and so could see what is happening at all times before making announcements by loudspeaker. The panel gave a better 'view' of movements than that obtained by looking out of the cubicle. Before 1927 announcements were made by megaphone. A signalling school opened in 1930.

Training signalmen.

THE CARRIAGE WORKS

The earliest railway building at York was the YNM two-road engine shed built in 1839; it soon was integrated into one of the Queen Street workshops. The YNM built the locomotive repair shop in Queen Street in 1842; small carriage repair and carriage painting shops were also built in Queen Street in 1849 – this was all closed in 1905 when the NER focused locomotive construction in Darlington. Older locomotives were upgraded at Queen Street; the works also carried out construction and repair of carriages and wagons and by 1864 was turning out 100 wagons per week. To cope with demand, wagon shops at Holgate, between Holgate and Leeman Roads, opened on a seventeen acre site in 1865 to build engines and tenders, extended in 1875. In 1876 output stood at 102 carriages, 2,387 wagons, 419 engines built with 2,865 carriages and 22,185 wagons repaired. The weekly pay bill was £2,500 for a workforce of 1,600. The typical carriage being built was 28 feet in length, weighing ten and a half tons, with four wheels, lit by gas.

The timber storage yard in the foreground with the apprentice school in the background, the light repair shop and the wash shed – photographed in 1964. Originally published in *The Life & Times of the York Carriage Works.*

The painters' day out to Wembley in 1928. Originally published in *The Life & Times of the York Carriage Works.*

Above Left: Lifting a five ton log of mahogany; originally published in *British Railways Magazine*, February 1948.

Above right: Cleaning the smoke box on the wet ash pit. Originally published in the *LNER Magazine*, July 1947.

Two views of the smiths' shop in the 1930s. Originally published in *The Life & Times of the York Carriage Works*.

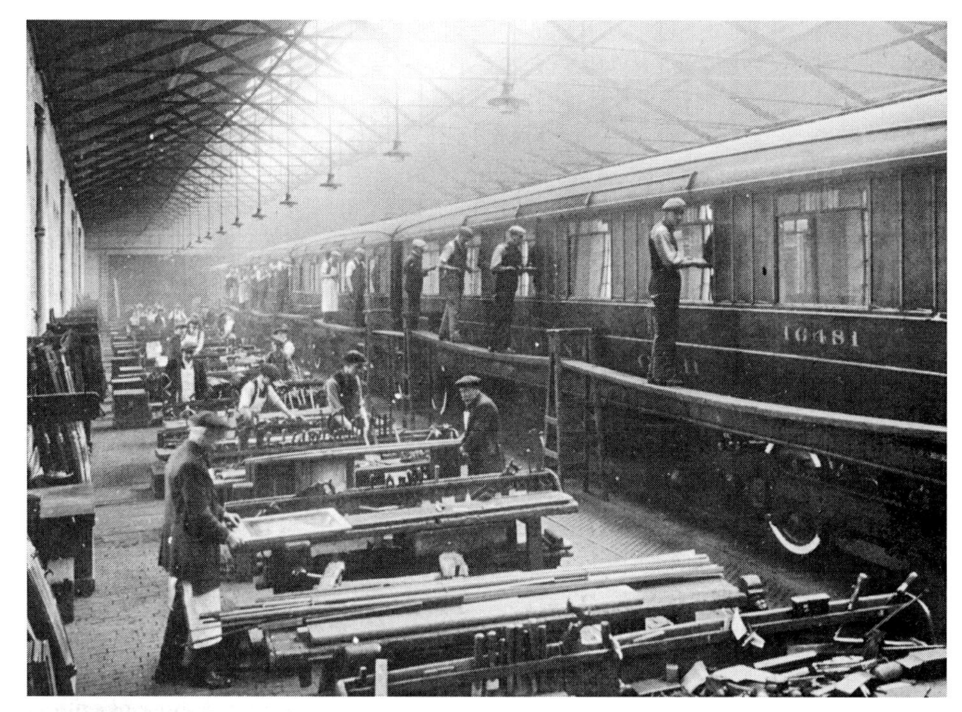

A 1925 shot of a Gresley Triplet Articulated Dining Set made up of an open first, open third and a full kitchen car in the centre for use on the East Coast main line. Originally published in *The Life & Times of the York Carriage Works*.

Above left: **Stuffing upholstery seats for third class compartments. Originally published in *British Railways Magazine*, February 1948.**

Above right: **Railway Coach restoration in 1972. ©*York Press*.**

Larger premises were built in 1884 around Holgate Road when it was decided to concentrate more carriage building at York; these were its busiest times, despite some work being transferred to Darlington: the 1890s and early 1900s were the Great Carriage Building Programme. Holgate was an integrated carriage building factory, with separate buildings for each process; by 1910 the works covered 45 acres. The site comprised two erecting shops; patternmakers shop; paint shop; fitting shop; machine shop; cylinder shop; coppersmiths' shop; boiler shop; blacksmiths' shop; foundry; and brass finishers. Typical carriages were now six or even twelve wheeled, and sixty feet in length. Cranes powered by electricity were purchased in 1896.

1885 saw the construction of the 5,000 gallon water tower standing on the coke store. The following year GT Andrews designed an 'engine stable' for the GNE: it accommodated six engines each with its own 24 feet stall accessed from a through track via a twelve feet diameter turntable. There was also a smithy used for minor repairs, obviating the need to send locomotives to Darlington.

Rates of pay in the 1890s were between £22, 6s 4½d and £25, 5d for a carriage and wagon examiner; £8, 9s 1¾d for a fifteen year old lad greaser rising to £17, 6 3½d at twenty-one years. In 1903 two Petrol Electric Autocars were built – two of the first examples of electric transmission in rail vehicles; the works also turned out charabancs and rolling stock for the North Tyneside electrification.

During the First World War, one marvelous production was the ambulance train made from existing carriage rolling stock; it comprised sixteen carriages and was known as 'Continental Ambulance Train Number 37'. This is covered in detail in the chapter on York railways during the two world wars.

Electricity for carriage lighting came on stream in 1915, necessitating the construction of electric and charging shops. A complete eight vehicle train was manufactured for the Director General of Transportations and his staff. It comprised accommodation for officers, sleeping quarters and dining facilities.

The carriage works built all of the coaching stock fleet of the NER, plus much of the East Coast Joint Stock and Great Northern and North-Eastern Joint Stock, as well as doing most of the NER's carriage repairs. The site comprised two main buildings, one for building and painting vehicles, the other housing the sawmill, frame and cabinet building, machine and brake shops. In addition there was a large timber drying building, and carriage washing facilities, a glass store and paint shop. The carriage works employed 1,500 people at one point.

In the 1930s the AH Peppercorn progressive system of construction was introduced whereby the carriage was moved through seven stages until completion. A fire in 1931 destroyed the wagon works sawmill; timber was moved allowing the building of a state of the art lifting shop. In 1932 the first self-contained buffet car was designed by Nigel Gresley for the Liverpool to Manchester line and built in York. It was a true café on wheels complete with bar and seating for twenty-two passengers.

The carriage works also built the bodies for the NER's fleet of buses, vans and lorries. This is a Maudsley from 1914, requisitioned by the War Department soon after completion and fitted with a lorry body. The bus bodies were restored after the war on Leyland chassis.

No 13 with pantographs down. Published in *Hennessey The Electric Railway that Never Was: York – Newcastle 1919.*

YORK'S ELECTRIC RAILWAYS

The electric railway that never was. That was the North Eastern Railway plan for the electrification of the East Coast Main Line between York and Newcastle in 1919 using a high speed electric locomotive designed by Sir Vincent Raven, chief mechanical engineer of the NER from 1910 to 1922; it was designated No. 13. The prototype locomotive was built at Darlington in May 1922 sporting six 300 hp electric motors. The wheels were 6 ft 8 in diameter, and the locomotive could achieve a speed of 65 mph on the level with a 450 ton train. On a test run on the Shildon line hauling nineteen vehicles weighing 460 tons the locomotive ascended a 1:200 incline at 58 mph which exceeded anything a steam locomotive could manage. Third rail and overhead power supply systems were both trialled at Strensall with some experiments using dummy collector shoes fitted to the bogie of a steam locomotive to assess the mechanical performance at speed. The overhead system was finally chosen.

The York – Newcastle electrification was a victim of the 1923 Grouping and shelved by the LNER, the new company which emerged from the Grouping; No. 13 was mothballed in the paint shop at Darlington. British Railways scrapped it in 1950. The public had to wait 75 years before the East Coast Main Line was eventually electrified in 1995.

Before that, between 1903 and 1904 York Carriage Works built the electric vehicles for the North Tyneside electrification project; around the same time they built two petrol-electric cars. After teething problems these two entered service in 1904 on the line between Scarborough and Filey; they were transferred to the Cawood Branch of the Selby line in 1908. Their daily routine also included a return trip to York. Road transport was becoming a real problem in the York area; in an attempt to confound this competition a 26 seater road bus was adapted to run on rails and in 1922 deployed on the York to Haxby and Strensall route, and on the lines to Poppleton, Earswick and Huntington, and Copmanthorpe. The buses were fitted with a radiator, a second driving position at the rear, and a door in the centre on each side with folding steps. Daily mileage was about 130 miles. Twelve months later in 1923 the rail-bus was moved to Selby and replaced by a 38 feet, seventeen ton new rail motor seating 40 passengers. Services were extended to Flaxton on the York, Haxby, Scarborough route and to Church Fenton after Copmanthorpe, with new services to Alne and Pocklington. The closure of the lines for passengers in the '30s saw the end of these services.

In the 1930s Sentinel steam railcars, Express Rail Motors, catered for summer traffic to Harrogate from York, stopping at Starbeck and Knaresborough. However, this had been anticipated in 1927 with a trial run on a circular route from York to Whitby and Scarborough and back. Three prototype diesel electric cars were trialled in 1931 between York and Harrogate.

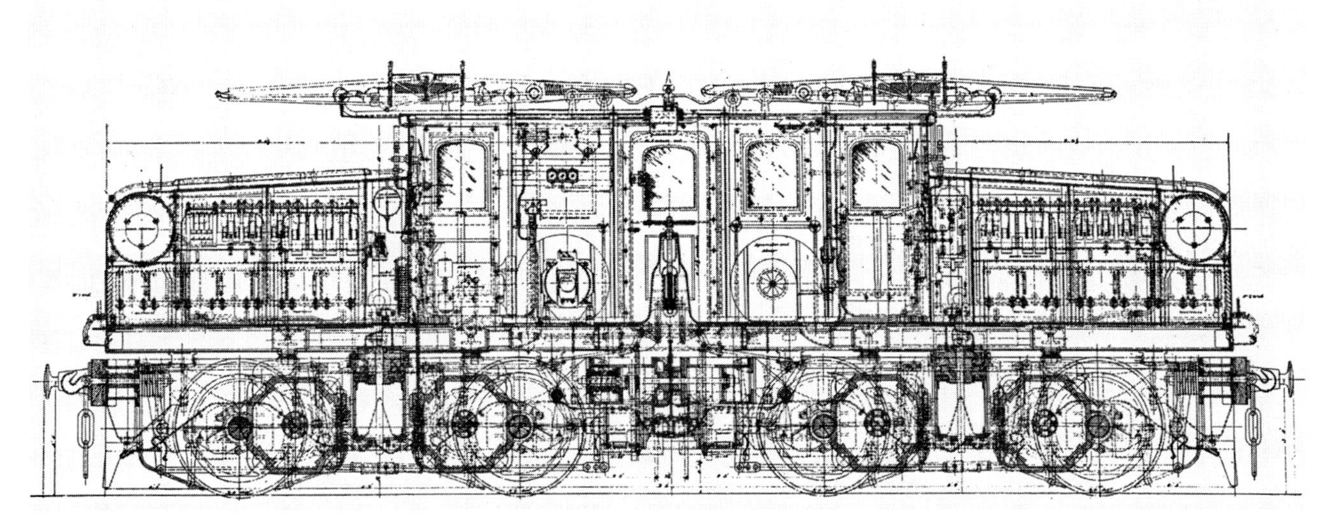

A plan of an electric locomotive. Published in Hennessey *The Electric Railway that Never Was: York – Newcastle 1919.*

YORK RAILWAY INSTITUTE

One of the less well known by-products of the Industrial Revolution was an upsurge in the demand for and provision of adult education:

> 'as a consequence of the introduction of machinery a class of workmen emerged to build, maintain and repair the machines on which the blessing of progress depended, at a time when population shifts and the dissolving influences of industrialization in the new urban areas, where these were concentrated, destroyed the inadequate old apprentice system and threw into relief the connection between material advancement and the necessity of education to take part in its advantages'.

This was before the Carnegie libraries and the introduction of public libraries. The Quakers were at the forefront of this movement with their highly organised adult schools and the sport and social facilities, and continuing education they provided, as a matter of course, for their workers in industrial villages such as New Earswick and Bournville. Mechanics' Institutes were important too, not least in York where the the York Institute of Mechanics opened. The aim of Mechanics' Institutes was to provide a technical education for the working man and for professionals: to *'address societal needs by incorporating fundamental scientific thinking and research into engineering solutions'*. They transformed science and technology education for the man in the street. The world's first opened in Edinburgh in 1821 as the School of Arts of Edinburgh, later to become Heriot-Watt University. This was followed later in 1821 by the Mechanics' Institute in Glasgow, which was founded on the site of the institution set up in 1800 by George Birkbeck and Anderson's University offering free lectures on arts, science and technical subjects. Birkbeck moved to London in 1804, and The London Mechanics' Institute was incorporated in 1823, later founding Birkbeck College. Liverpool opened in July 1823 and Manchester (later to become UMIST) in 1824. By 1850, there were over 700 Institutes in the UK and abroad, many of which developed into libraries, colleges and universities.

Mechanics' Institutes provided free lending libraries and also offered lectures, laboratories, and occasionally, as with Glasgow, a museum. The York Institute had its stimulus from a Whig newspaper article about the London Society for the Diffusion of Useful Knowledge. The Tories, on the other hand, were paranoid and suspicious of the *'efforts to awaken the dormant powers of the mind in the middling, but more especially in the lower classes of society'*. Nevertheless, York opened in 1827 in Bedern with a membership of 272; appeals for books for the library produced over 500 by the end of the year. The Institute struggled, though, and, as elsewhere, did not hold the attraction for the working classes the founders hoped it would. Indeed, the 1834 writers of the annual report were naively indignant about the local lack of support for an Institute that they foolishly said was *'designed and adapted to check the progress of Frivolity, Dissipation and Vice'* – so unintentionally aligning it with the Quaker supported York Society for the Prevention and Discouragement of Profaneness and Vice (lewdness, brothel-keeping, intoxication, swearing and Sabbath-breaking). This, in turn, was lampooned as a society for the suppression of the *'vice of persons whose income does not exceed £500 per annum'*.

The institute's Queen Street building still stands today.

The Institute was not a success for the simple reason that its agenda were at odds with the needs of its students: *'values and ideals which were totally out of touch with the reality of the lives of its students. Much of its curriculum was beyond the comprehension and ability of most of its pupils'*. In 1838 the Institute changed its name to reflect a new focus and became the York Institute of Popular Science and Literature housed in St Saviourgate. Lectures became more populist; they included phrenology and one on Phineas Taylor Barnum in 1855. Musical entertainment was introduced in 1846. The evening classes, though, were always a success: Society of Arts examinations were taken from 1851 leading to the opening of the Institute School of Art in 1881 in King Street; City and Guilds technical examinations and commercial examinations of the Yorkshire Union of Mechanics' Institutes were introduced. These paved the way for the Institute to transform itself into a technical college which is what it became when it moved into a building in the newly-built Clifford Street in 1885.

In 1889 York Railway Institute was opened on the back of all this on the site of the Railway Tavern to provide educational and recreational activities for the railway workers of York. It survives and thrives today with over 3,000 members in activities ranging from sailing and golf, judo, dance, pilates, yoga, brass bands and theatre to chess and dominoes. The site was also significant in that it removed one of the temptations open to workers who arrived at their benches after 'a swift half'; there were, of course, many other pubs in which to imbibe in the vicinity but it was a start. Another attempt at spreading temperance came in the shape of Temperance Coffee Wagons shops run by the Quaker York Adult Schools between 1871 and 1880; one was strategically stationed outside the works at Queen Street. 'Mechanics and others going to their labours in the morning' could get coffee to go for ½d a cup Monday to Friday with a meal deal bun at the same price.

The opening of the original Railway Library and Reading Room Institution was celebrated with a grand tea in the Lecture Hall in Goodramgate with music by the band of the 7th Hussars (ironically, it seems, on a George Hudson scale of grandness). It had as its model the York Institute for Popular Science, Art and Literature and had as its aim to help younger railway employees 'to employ their energies better than by wandering about the streets or resorting to places which would neither improve their minds nor their pockets'. Other such NER Institutes existed by now at Shildon (1833, the world's first), Gateshead (1857), Darlington (1858); Forth (Newcastle), Blyth and Dairycoates (Hull).

Self-improvement and education were paramount. In the lofty and somewhat garbled words of George Leeman, the mission statement for the Institute was a place in which 'the men, whose brawny arms and strong muscle and mechanical skill work out that great and important agent of the present century to which this country is indebted for the pre-eminent position it holds in the scale of nations'. To that end the Institute was equipped with a library and a reading room with books, periodicals and York's weekly newspapers; dailies were not published in the city until later in 1874. Initially, most of the books were donated by members, friends and shareholders of the NER amounting to an impressive stock of 9,223 at the closure of the old library in 1889; this formed the basis of the new library which was in the Sack Warehouse in the old station yard. 24,000 loans were issued each year to 512 members.

The subscription for the Institute was 1d a week. The new Institute dining hall seated 400 diners with heating-up facilities for workers who brought breakfast and lunches from home; there was a smoke room ' for those who wished to indulge in the doubtful enjoyment of smoking' and a games room for cards, bagatelle, chess and billiards, and five classrooms, as well as the luxury of lavatories which the old building never had. The new building continued the mission 'to convey information and spread education on a variety of subjects'. 'Improving subjects' formed the basis of the lectures. A branch of the NER Bank of Deposits opened there. The Institute was to some extent a working man's Assembly Rooms, but with a formal educational aspect. No alcohol was allowed on the premises although tea and coffee were. This comes as no surprise as the founder president, Henry Tennant, was a Quaker and a prominent figure in the NER Temperance Union. Three years after Tennant's retirement the Institute was clearly leaking members to other non dry 'clubs' in the city.

In 1889 1,444 railway workers joined the Institute within six months of opening; 231 of these enrolled in the educational classes; in order of popularity they were: shorthand, machine construction and drawing, French, free-hand and model drawing, applied mechanics and book-keeping. For the less able there were foundation classes in the three 'r's. Book prizes were liberally used for motivation and as incentives. Another attractive incentive was that fees were waived for those students who attended 20 lectures in one subject and sat the examination. The connection with York Institute of Popular Science led to the sensible arrangement where neither would duplicate the classes of the other. Accordingly, the Railway Institute offered metallurgy, mechanics, steam and the steam engine, electricity and magnetism and chemistry; the Micklegate Bar School was hired to cope with the extra numbers wanting to take these evening classes. Under the terms of the Technical Instruction Act of 1889 the Institute was now obliged to throw its doors open to

The ladies' gymnastic class in 1948. Photograph by Breda Walker (nee Gardner) and published in *Opportunity of Leisure*.

the public. This offered a revenue-earning opportunity: the general public paid 5s per class while railway personnel were charged 2s. By 1907 educational class enrolments were at a high of 613 and this at a time when the overall membership of the Institute fell to a low of 872 in 1905. There were also useful classes in first aid and in fire fighting when the NER had its own fire brigade based in York.

In 1889 the library at the Institute was the only accessible public library in York, which goes a long way to explaining its popularity. The Minster Library was academic and specialised; the Subscription Library demanded an expensive entrance fee of ten guineas and an annual membership charge of 1s 6d; circulating libraries and the York Institute library seemed to have been the preserve of the middle classes. The Corporation free library did not open until 1893. The 9,223 inaugural collection of books was very soon complemented by a further 543 volumes: half of the books were novels *'but the cheap sensationals were eschewed, whilst prominence is given to the best authors such as Lytton, Scott, Eliot, Dickens and Trollope'*; science, history, geography, travel and biography sections were strong. Lenders were unable to select from shelves, as we are used to doing today; instead, a list of six books had to be handed in, selected from the catalogue. In the first six months an astonishing 23,715 books were borrowed from the new library – twice that at the old library.

The reading room was open from 8.00 am to 10.00 pm; at the end of the First World War it offered 23 daily newspapers both local and national, 58 weekly papers and 45 monthly magazines on a wide range of subjects. One of its international papers, *The Detroit Free Press* must have been much in demand.

Lectures too were diverse, some may say perverse, in subject. Over the years they were often augmented with magic lantern images; the more riveting included 'A Temperance Tour Around the World' by Fielden Thorpe, the Quaker head of Bootham School; 'How I Walked to Monte Carlo' by the Rev. AN Cooper; and, much more interesting, 'The Volcanoes of Central America' by the distinguished York vulcanologist, Tempest Anderson. The York Railway Lecture and Debating Society was formed in 1904 and was extremely popular with debates on railway organisation and management.

Despite the aspirations of Alexander Kaye Butterworth (General Manager of the NER and President of the Institute) at the 1907 AGM when he asserted that *'billiards are good, study is better'*, by the 1920s the educational role of the Institute had diminished in the face of demand for more recreational activities. Nevertheless, the library collection was still over 11,000 volumes in 1929, reduced after culls to get rid of *'unsuitable tomes'*: some of these were sent to the York Military Hospital or inflicted on the newly opened railway institute at Sunderland. The *'insatiable demand for thrillers'* continued with only 120 out of the 1,035 new books in 1931 being non fiction. Around 1930 members were borrowing on average 35 books in a year. Library shelving and free access self-selection were introduced at last in 1921.

1926 saw the redundant carriage-building shops on the Queen Street site converted into a large gymnasium. Boxing was particularly popular; in 1920 the York Railway Institute Golf Club was formed with a nine hole course at Hob Moor. Membership was restricted to 200 'railway employees' and 25 'outside members'. By 1939 membership stood at nearly 4,000. The demise of the educational role coincided with the new obligations imposed on corporations to provide educational facilities for all of its citizens. There ended a fine, prestigious and successful service of further education provided by York railways. In the end, the 234 ladies got their own reading room, away from the men; they must have been so grateful to share the nine magazines and periodicals specially stocked for them – out of a total of 74.

YORK RAILWAYS IN THE WARS

The Sailors'and Soldiers' Buffet at York Station. Originally published in an issue of *NER Magazine* in 1915.

North Eastern Railway Maudslay and Leyland trucks converted from buses and charabancs at the York Carriage and Wagon Works for the war effort and destined for the War Department. Originally published in an issue of *NER Magazine* in 1914.

THE FIRST WORLD WAR

At the outbreak of war all the main line railways fell under the control of the Railway Executive Committee, thus effectively nationalising them. British railways played an extraordinary role of biblical proportions just in the week from August 10th to 17th 1914: 68,847 men, 21,523 horses, 166 guns, 2,446 vehicles, 1,368 bicycles and 2,550 tonnes of baggage and stores were shipped from the UK to France by rail. 184,475 railway workers joined up while many thousands more stayed in the UK to build the vehicles and to keep the railways running. About a third of railway staff were called up and freight tonnage doubled; passenger traffic was increased with the movements of service personnel and rolling stock was requisitioned.

In York, Castle Yard became an internment camp for aliens with room for 40,000 apparently, as did a field in Leeman Road. The Cattle Market became a horse depot. The military requisitioned the De Grey Rooms, the Exhibition Hall and the Railway Institute; Knavesmire was a drill ground; an aerodrome was built at Copmanthorpe; 700 Belgian refugees were lodged in private houses in New Earswick and York; a canteen for travelling troops opened on York Railway Station; VAD hospitals opened in Clifford Street and at St John's College; stranded soldiers were given supper, bed and breakfast in the Assembly Rooms – 435 in one record night with over 100,000 all told. A munitions factory was opened in Queen Street in two sheds hired from the NER employing 1,000, mainly

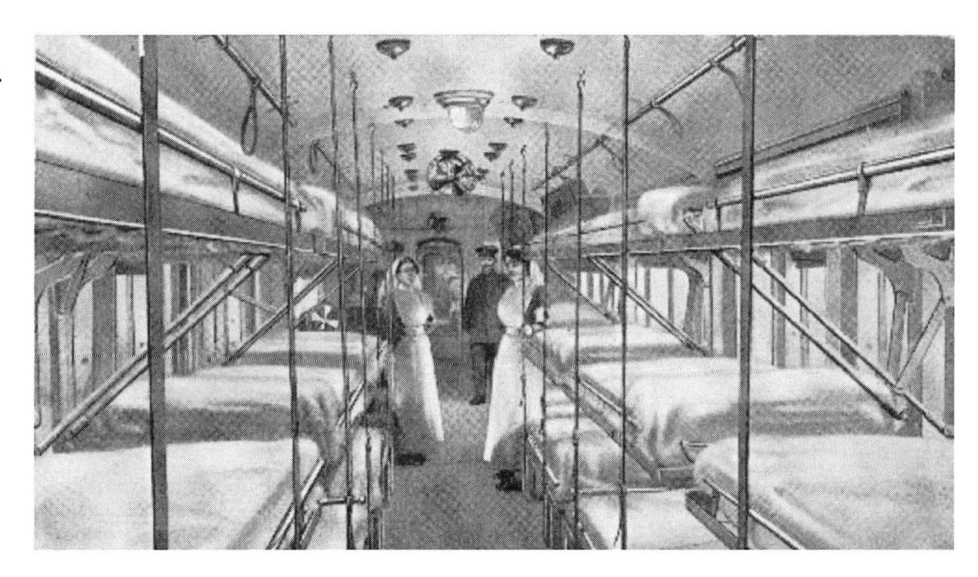
A ward car built by the Caledonian Railway Company.

women and girls. By the second week of the war registered aliens filled the Castle Prison with more held in a property in Leeman Road. Just before 1914 nearly two thirds of York's NER labour force was engaged in running the railway while the rest were employed at the carriage works. Of York's total 37,000 labour force 10,000 worked either in confectionery or railway related work. A further 1,600 were already in the army.

As elsewhere the streets of York were alive with military personnel, or with those aspiring to be military personnel, rushing hither and thither. The recruitment campaign, though, in York was not met with the gusto and alacrity seen elsewhere. Nevertheless, regiments marching through the city or training on the Knavesmire were cheered and offered food. *The Yorkshire Herald* in September reported that almost 5,000 NER staff had signed up, thus bucking the local trend, although many of these did not actually live in the city itself. Whatever, over 2,000 sadly never came back. Like Leetham's who promised full pay for the duration to the families of mobilised workers, the NER offered financial protection, on application, to families of servicemen. As with other large local employers like Rowntree and Leetham, the NER met with enthusiasm the call for distress relief, urging workers to contribute 1d a week for every 10s earned. By the end of the month the fund totalled £3,700.

York and its surrounding area would have been a fertile source of recruits for the North Eastern Railway Battalion – 17th (Pioneer) Btn. Northumberland Fusiliers, despite the numbers of NER York staff who had already joined up. In September 1914 a circular asking for 11,000 volunteers elicited a response from over 30,000 hopefuls within three days. Recruitment duties were shared between the York and Newcastle Railway Institutes. The pioneer corps status was an obvious and appropriate reflection of the construction and engineering skills of the NER recruits, although the battalion would also serve as a standard infantry unit as required. After training in the UK the Battalion sailed for France in November 1915, destined for the Somme Valley. Much of their work involved maintaining trenches and dug outs with rewiring, drainage, building and reconstruction. Their railway laying broke all records. On December 23rd the first casualty, Teddy Marsden, was killed by a shell. The supporting role at the Somme offensive in July 1916 cost the Battalion eleven dead and 86 wounded. Loos was next. Further details on the battalion's activities throughout the war can be found in Rob Langham's fascinating *The North East Railway in The First World War.*

The outbreak of war led to the cancellation of summer excursions from August Bank Holiday (then held at the beginning of the month), to free up the railway system for mass troop movements. Interestingly, *The Press* reported that the there was no violent reaction to this news and that the people accepted it all quite philosophically. Locally, flower shows at Poppleton and Heworth were well supported. At the station on the Bank Holiday there were reportedly over 100 special trains carrying reservists to various units while excursion traffic to Scarborough was down from the usual 29 trains to eight. The resort reported a 15,000 drop in visitors and an air of 'uneasiness and anxiety'.

The catering facilities on York Station were challenging to say the least as hundreds of thousands of servicemen passed through on their way home for leave or back to their units. They would have been hungry and thirsty, irascible and tired, waiting endlessly for connections. The existing buffet closed at 5:30pm, the *Yorkshire Evening Press* reported shabby service. This shocking situation could not be allowed to continue, so on November 15th 1915, a Soldiers' and Sailors' Canteen was set up on what was then platform three – now platform one – comprising two carriages donated by the North Eastern Railway serving tea, coffee and snacks to uniformed servicemen. It was run by volunteers and was open 24 hours a day, seven days a week until it closed on May 23rd 1919. Over that time it served four and a half million servicemen – an average of 18,000 every week. The dedication and selflessness of the volunteers was conspicuous. This comment on a passenger's experience at York Station in the middle of the night published in the *NER Magazine* for November 1918 clearly shows why:

> 'Service men predominate but civilians of both sexes awaiting train connections help to swell the numbers. Arriving trains disgorge not only sleepy passengers, but incredibly large quantities of parcels, newspapers and mails. But what struck him most was the unselfish service given by the ladies at the soldiers' and sailors' canteen where business was very brisk indeed'.

Patriotic generosity as shown in the distress relief efforts described above prevailed throughout the war. In a letter published in *The North East Railway Magazine* in late 1918 and anticipating the NER War Memorial at York, Mr F Ascough, Traffic Foreman at Hartlepool, pleaded the case for '*a fitting tribute to our lost fellow-workers. How about a memorial placed at a good centre like York?*'. On May 10th 1918 four services were held to commemorate the NER dead: at York Minster, Newcastle Cathedral, Holy Trinity Hull, and at St. Mary's Gateshead. Relatives were invited and fellow staff given the day off to attend. Special trains were, of course, laid on to cope with the huge numbers of mourners involved: 6,000 attended the York service alone.

Overall, the war was a commercial success for the NER which was more than busy with military related movements in one form or another. The so-called halcyon days pre-war had yielded dividends of up to 7%, a figure seen again in 1917 despite lower yields in the early years of the war. The provision of 24,000 troop trains and movement of over 5 million tons of government supplies were obviously major contributary factors. The Railway Executive Committee learned much from the unification it imposed during the war, leading to the 1921 Railways Act and the grouping of the railway companies into the 'Big Four'.

The carriage works were extremely busy and significant contributors to the war effort, as might be expected. Horse-drawn vehicles were particularly important; these were augmented by 984 general service wagons for the Army Service Corps, Officers Mess

Guerre 1914 – this postcard was published in Paris; it shows RAMC soldiers having just unloaded casualties at a French port for on shipment to the UK.

Carts and 412 General Service Limbers. York also helped the French army when it built 400 20-ton covered wagons which ran on French railways. Less obviously, 1,850 stretchers came out of York, entrenching tools, pack saddles for artillery horses and 400 clarifying reels for use in water purification. The construction of tank transporters must have been an unexpected contract; the revolutionary 20-ton mobile war machine needed a very special vehicle for transportation and the railways were an obvious answer to at least part of the challenge. Existing flat wagons were inadequate and unsuitable: they could only be loaded at the ends and they could not bear the weight of a tank. York produced 40 of the new RECTANKS, themselves weighing 35 tons with the crucial design feature that they could be loaded from the side. So good were they that they were used in the Second World War as well.

One production which rolled out of York Carriage Works was the ambulance train made from existing carriage rolling stock; it comprised sixteen carriages and was known as '*Continental Ambulance Train Number 37*'. It was 890 feet 8 inches long and weighed 465 tons when loaded, without a locomotive. Painted khaki it bore the Geneva Red Cross painted on the window panels and frames on each of the carriages on both sides. This mobile field station featured

- A brake and infectious lying down car carrying a guard and eighteen patients in two self-contained sections, each with bathroom and own water supply to prevent cross-infection.
- A staff car occupied by four RAMC officers and four St John Ambulance nurses – it featured two mess rooms, one for the officers, the other for the nurses; three bedrooms for the officers and two for the nurses, one of which contained a bunk bed – all bedrooms had a wardrobe, book shelf, table, chair, net racks and a steam heated radiator; the nurses' toilet contained a shower and hot and cold running water; that of the officers was in the Kitchen Car which accommodated 20 cases and three cooks who lived in a single room with a three bed bunk.
- The kitchen car was fitted out with an Army Dixie Range Oven, copper boiler and two sinks; as well as the officers' lavatory this coach also had a pantry for the officers and room for 20 sick officers.
- Eight ward cars constituted as one sick officers lying down car, three ordinary lying down cars and four ordinary ward cars – each car contained 36 beds (or 'cots'as they were termed) arranged on each side of the carriage – for safety, each bed was fitted with two leather straps, the mattresses were filled with wood fibre, the two pillows with white flock; for extra comfort there was an ash tray and a bracket for a spitting cup; there was a lavatory at one end and a sink at the other end of the carriage.
- A pharmacy car comprising a dispensary and a treatment room with operating table, portable electric lamp and facilities for sterilization, an office, a pantry for 'medical comforts', and a linen room.
- An infectious sitting car with room for 56 sitting up cases and fourteen lying down divided into seven compartments accessed by a side corridor. Three of these were 'specially fitted for Mental Cases' fitted with iron bars over the windows and swing doors separating it from the rest of the train, a lavatory at one end and a pantry at the other.
- A kitchen and mess room for three more cooks; the two mess rooms were for the use of NCOs and for 'other men'.
- A personnel car for 33 medical orderlies.
- A brake and stores car with another guard and his living room, and three store rooms, a meat safe with electric fan and chopping board.

Overall, the ambulance car could carry between 445 and 659 patients and staff, depending on how it was configured. Obviously, good ventilation, light and infection control were paramount; there were electric fans everywhere with extra ones for gassed patients. To promote hygiene, round corners were used and the toilets, wash rooms and treatment room all had concrete floors. The kitchen was floored with lead while other areas were covered in linoleum. A smooth ride was essential for the injured: to that end the train had bolster, side bearing and auxiliary springs on the four wheeled bogies which ran on 'patent cushioned wheels'.

Two beds arranged for sitting up cases; this one was built in Swindon in 1915 at the GWR works.

In the early days of the war the first British ambulance trains were rudimentary, to say the least, consisting of French goods wagons with straw strewn on the floor. By August 1914 things started to improve when the Royal Army Medical Corps (RAMC) was given three locomotives, some goods wagons and carriages. These were converted and divided into three 'trains' comprising wards, surgical dressing rooms and dispensaries and were designated British Ambulance Trains 1, 2 and 3 respectively. During 1915 they carried 461,844 patients.

RAMC conversions continued up to train No. 11. It was decided that a number of 'standard' trains should be built by various British railway companies to War Office specifications. In November 1914, the first specially built medical train was sent out from the UK designated No. 12. No train was given number 13; the last to arrive in France was No. 43. The UK Flour Millers' Association presented the Red Cross with two ambulance trains, specially-built and equipped, constructed by the Great Western and Great Eastern Railways. The movement of the injured from the trains soon became highly efficient: Boulogne was the main port for embarkation for the wounded and it is recorded that on one occasion it took only nineteen minutes to detrain 123 casualties. The main disembarkation points in the UK were Dover and Southampton. Over the course of the war, Dover dealt with 1,260,506 casualties, unloaded 4,076 boats and loaded 7, 781 ambulance trains. The patients were then sent by one of the 20 'home standard' ambulance trains, or by an emergency ambulance train, to a receiving station, where they were transferred to road vehicles, usually by volunteer first aiders, which took them to their destination hospital. There were 196 receiving stations in the UK including one at York.

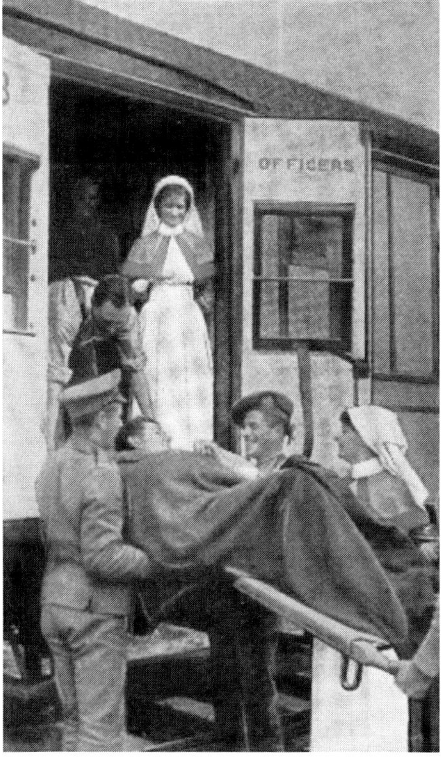

An official Canadian card showing members of the Queen Alexandra's Imperial Military Nursing Service with their distinctive scarlet capes. In August 1914 there were only 300 QAs serving with the British Army; by the end of the year there were 2,223 and there were over 10,400 at the end of the war.

York's *Number 37* was one of 42 British Ambulance Trains pressed into service overseas, mainly on the Western Front but three were also deployed in Italy and one in Egypt. A further 22 saw action in the UK while the American Expeditionary Force used nineteen more conversions, including one being built in York, identical to *Number 37*, which was unfinished when the Armistice was signed. Before it left for the front in 1917 *Number 37* was used as an exhibition which was attended by 36,404 people touring the train and raising £1,802, 5s for the Red Cross.

The tragedy and pathos of the circumstances surrounding the work of the ambulance trains is admirably captured by Phillip Gibbs of the *Daily Chronicle* after seeing an ambulance train near the village of Choques filling up with men suffering all manner of trauma. The first to board were thousands of *"lightly wounded"*, he said, who *"crowded the carriages, leaned out of the windows with their bandaged heads and arms, shouting at friends they saw in the other crowds. The spirit of victory, and of lucky escape, uplifted these lads...And now they were going home to bonny Scotland, with a wound that would take some time to heal"*. Next were stretcher cases *"from which no laughter came"*. One young Londoner, *"was so smashed about the face"*, reported Gibbs, *"that only his eyes were uncovered between the bandages, and they were glazed with the first film of death"*. Another young soldier *"had his jaw blown clean away. A splendid boy of the Black Watch, was but a living trunk"*, he said, *"both his arms and legs were shattered and would be one of those who go about in boxes on wheels"*. A group of blinded men, *"were led to the train by wounded comrades, 'groping', very quiet, thinking of a life of darkness ahead of them..."*

We get an equally harrowing picture of the practical difficulties of working on an ambulance train from the *Anonymous Diary of a Nursing Sister on the Western Front*:

> "October 25 couldn't write last night: the only thing was to try and forget it all. It has been an absolute hell of a journey – there is no other word for it. ...They were bleeding faster than we could cope with it; and the agony of getting them off the stretchers on to the top bunks is a thing to forget. A train of cattle trucks came in from Rouen with all the wounded as they were picked up without a spot of dressing on any of their wounds, which were septic and full of straw and dirt. The matron, a medical officer, and some of them got hold of some dressings and went round doing what they could in the time, and others fed them. Then the [censored] – got their Amiens wounded into cattle trucks on mattresses, with Convent pillows, and has a twenty hours' journey with them in frightful smells and dirt ... they'd been travelling already for two days."

THE SECOND WORLD WAR

The Second World War also saw the deployment of ambulance trains to transfer the wounded to the many temporary and permanent UK Military Hospitals. The train companies supplied and converted ambulance trains sanctioned by the Railway Executive Committee. There were about 30 or so ambulance trains in operation at the beginning of the war.

In 1943 there were 544,715 railway men and 105, 703 railway women throughout Britain; 102,984, mainly men, had left the railways for service in the forces. The railways were amongst the first to form their Home Guard units (LDV) with hundreds of thousands volunteering. Railway personnel were particularly in demand for work in the Docks Groups, Movement Control Units, and the Railway Construction companies attached to the Royal Engineers. Before the war there were 26,000 women employed on the railways, mainly in clerical jobs or as carriage cleaners, office cleaners, crossing keepers, cooks or

Women at work in the war; originally published in Facts about British Railways in Wartime published in 1943 by the BR Press Office.

The Home Guard protecting York, on Lendal Bridge. Originally published in Leo Kessler's and Eric Taylor's *The York Blitz 1942.*

waiting room attendants. As the war progressed they took on and were trained in a wide range of functions left vacant by men. Interestingly, they were paid the same wages, after an agreed time, as the men whose positions they filled. Women turned their hands to all manner of jobs, including loaders and porters, oilers, greasers and firelighters, on track maintenance and as coppersmiths, welders, concrete mixers and turners.

Restaurant cars were withdrawn for the duration, replaced by mobile platform trolleys; this was totally inadequate for larger stations such as York where guard rails had to be used to fend off the clamouring mobs desperate for food and drink and to encourage orderly queuing. Trolleys also plied their trade up and down the length of the trains. At York a removable buffet was pioneered in 1943; its success led to similar arrangements at Darlington and Newcastle.

In York as elsewhere many companies were transformed into completely different companies in support of the war effort – Rowntree's 'became' County Industries Ltd – or else they hosted other war manufacturers: Rowntree, for example, manufactured *Oxford Marmalade* on behalf of Frank Cooper Ltd. The brief for County Industries Ltd was mainly to produce shell and mine fuses in the *Smarties* block. In addition, 300 clerks of the Royal Army Pay Corps moved in as did York firm Cooke, Troughton & Simms for the manufacture of military optical instruments. Out of the Cream Department came *National Milk Cocoa, Ryvita, Household Milk* and dried egg. The Card Box Mill swapped production of fancy boxes for supplies for the RASC, Northern Command. Part of the Dining Block became a refuge for blitzed families, notably in the aftermath of the 1942 Baedeker Raid; a VAD hospital with 100 or so beds occupied the rest of the building. There was also a nursery to allow mothers of young children to come to work. At any one time 60 children were in occupation; cots were made by the work's joiners and the orchard became the playground. York carriage works too was at the forefront of war effort manufacturing.

In addition to the regular work of repairing bomb damaged stock the York carriages works produced Blackburn Botha (General Reconnaissance and Torpedo) bombers, and Horsa gliders main planes and parts from laminated spruce and ply wood. High speed launches for the Royal Navy were an important part of the work; in December 1944 the building in which they were made was destroyed in an accidental fire, caused by sparks from the boiler house chimney. York built six experimental 60 ton pontoon rafts – the purpose of which remained a secret – pontoon floats, battery boxes and a sixteen feet motor dinghy. The lifting shop built bridges, Bailey Bridges, shore transoms and booms. Other work included the manufacture of gun emplacements, tank parts, and Lancaster bomber trailing edge wings which were shipped to Chadderton near Manchester for assembly. During the war much of the work was done by women who made up 15% of the workforce across a wide

The Home Guard on the city walls. Originally published in Leo Kessler's and Eric Taylor's *The York Blitz 1942*.

WAAFS, later WRAFS, marching in York. Originally published in Leo Kessler's and Eric Taylor's *The York Blitz 1942*.

German POWs arriving at York Station in 1943 – probably heading on to the camp on the Knavesmire. Originally published in Leo Kessler's and Eric Taylor's *The York Blitz 1942*.

range of occupations; they worked shifts of up to 69 hours a week. Teak stocks were frozen by the Admiralty early in the war and supplies of mahogany ran out with spruce being used instead. A Home Guard unit was set up commanded by the works manager using the paint and trimming shops as a drill hall and rifle range.

During the Baedeker raid one of a stick of bombs landed on the main arterial line at the carriage works, but failed to explode. The bomb kept sinking in the sandy soil, making it very difficult for the bomb disposal squad to defuse it over a number of days. The carriage works staff held a collection for the army staff. In December 1944 the main carriage building shop was razed to the ground but a new, leading edge shop rose in its place, commonly regarded as the best in Britain. In 1947 and 1949 *The Flying Scotsman* and *The Junior Scotsman* carriages were built here.

The story of the Baedeker Raid and its tragic and destructive impact on York Station is well known. By April 1942 York had received 780 alerts but luckily only a few people had been killed – on three separate occasions when stray bombs had been dropped probably by German aircraft lightening their loads on the way from other targets. An indication of York's apparent immunity was that the public shelters were barely used: a large shelter near the city centre had two doors, both of which carried a notice saying – 'Key on other door' – the key was in fact in a small glass case at the end of the shelter, with a notice asking people to break the glass to obtain the key – the glass remained unbroken several days after the Baedeker Raid.

The wholesale destruction by the RAF of the beautiful medieval towns of Lübeck and Rostock, shocked not just the Germans. Goebbels was unnerved, clearly seeing the consequence for Germany and the morale of the German people:

> 'the English air raids have increased in scope and importance; if they can be continued for weeks on the same lines, they might conceivably have a demoralizing effect on the population'. After Rostock he said 'the air raid… was more devastating than those before. Community life there is practically at an end.. the situation is in some sections catastrophic…seven tenths of the city have been destroyed.. more than 100,000 people had to be evacuated… there was, in fact, panic'. Hitler was outraged, demanding retaliation of the most destructive kind : 'preference is to be given to those where attacks are likely to have the greatest possible effect on civilian life'. Besides raids on ports and industry, terror attacks of a retaliatory nature (Vergeltungsangriffe) were to be carried out on towns other than London. After Bath, the second of the retaliations, Hitler's plan was to 'repeat these raids night after night until the English are sick and tired of terror attacks... cultural centres, health resorts and civilian centres must be attacked...there is no other way of bringing the English to their senses. They belong to a class of human beings with whom you can only talk after you have first knocked out their teeth'.

We owe the tag these raids were given, "Baedeker Raids", to German Foreign Office propagandist Baron Gustav Braun von Stumm, who reputedly exclaimed *"We shall go out and bomb every building in Britain marked with three stars in the Baedeker Guide,"* the popular and authoritative travel guides. Exeter was the first to be hit over two nights (April 23rd-25th) causing over 80 fatalities. Bath was next (25th -27th) with 400 casualties. On the following night the *Luftwaffe* hit Norwich, dropping more than 90 tons of bombs and causing 67 deaths. York was next on the night of April 28th-29th. One week later, they were back over Exeter, resulting in heavy damage and 164 deaths. The next night they attacked Cowes, a place of both cultural and military significance, being the home of the J. Samuel White shipyard. Norwich was bombed again.

Overall, a total of 1,637 civilians were killed and 1,760 injured in the raids, and over 50,000 houses were destroyed. Famous buildings flattened or damaged included York's Guildhall and the Bath Assembly Rooms, but in general these fine cities were very lucky; the cathedrals of Norwich, Exeter and Canterbury and York Minster remained, by and large, unscathed.

For the York raid, civil defence records tell us that 65 high explosive bombs fell and *'practically all did damage to a greater or lesser degree'*. Twenty-four UXBs were reported: eight were exploded, six were dealt with or were to be dealt with, and ten were false reports. Fourteen clusters of incendiary bombs fell.

CASUALTIES WITHIN THE CITY

	Male	Female	Children	Total
CIVILIAN				
Dead	23	39	8	70
Seriously injured.	42	43	7	92
Slightly injured.	68	41	4	113
CIVIL DEFENCE PERSONNEL.				
Dead	4	-	-	4

Damage in the vicinity of the station was reported as follows:

North St. Rowntree's old warehouse	incendiary bombs	burnt out
Railway Station entrance.	high explosive/ incendiary bombs	
King's Manor	incendiary bombs	fire
Exhibition Buildings	high explosive/ incendiary bombs	fire
Rest Garden Station Road.	high explosive	

York Railway Station was an obvious strategic target, with its prodigious war effort work at the carriage works and its role as a hub for trains carrying troops, supplies and equipment to depots and barracks all over the country, not least to the nation's ports. At around 2.30 am the flares, bombs and incendiaries were released from 20 Junker 88s and Heinkel IIIs. The destruction began when a stick of HE bombs fell either side of the railway bridge linking Bootham Terrace and Grosvenor Terrace; in the sky *Oberfeldwebel* Hans Fruehauf soon picked out the railway station and remembered the briefing officer's command to *'obliterate the signalling system and there won't be much leaving Hull for Murmansk for the next weeks'*. With terrible bad timing the blacked out 10.15 pm express from King's Cross pulled into the station crammed with passengers – military and civilian – worn out after a five hour journey. The loudspeaker urgently warned them to evacuate but few initially did, encumbered in many cases by full kit and weapons. A 250 pound bomb changed all that when it smashed through the station roof landing on platforms 2 and 3, destroying the parcels office, and the 10.15 from King's Cross, the *Night Scotsman*, which had pulled up at platform 9. Staff rushed to help: assistant stationmaster Lyon, driver Stevans from Gateshead, two shunters and an anonymous soldier managed to

The damage done to the roof, and the Parcels Office and Booking Office, both of which were totally destroyed.

The totally destroyed Sir Ralph Wedgwood.

uncouple the train from both ends so that fifteen of the 20 carriages could be safely separated; the middle five were left burning beyond recovery. In another shunter signalman Simpson, who had escaped from his damaged box, manoeuvred a further 20 coaches and the flaming parcels van to safety. Meanwhile, women porters were kicking burning debris onto the relative safety of the rails while blazing furniture was dumped into a nearby moat. The day's takings were salvaged, deposited in William Green's Wellington boot and removed to the Royal Station Hotel next door. The fateful HE bomb that shattered the roof was followed by a stick of incendiaries, one of which smashed into the lamp room and the 500 gallons of paraffin stored there. The lamp room, parcels office, booking office and stationmaster's office were burnt to the ground in the ensuing conflagration.

Further north the line was blocked when a bomb exploded between Clifton and Skelton. This, of course, caused a problem for the evacuation of the stranded passengers to all destinations north, particularly as there was nothing for them to eat at York and, more crucially, the BBC told the world, and German intelligence, that the Minster had been

The plaque in memory of William Milner.

spared. A repeat raid was fully expected, and was indeed launched. The RAF, however, had heard the BBC news as well and shot down or dispersed the attack aircraft over the English coast; the second raid was aborted. The previous night's unfortunate passengers were packed onto a fourteen coach train which set off circuitously for the main line at Northallerton via Selby, Harrogate and Ripon.

A plaque on platform 8a at York Station commemorates another hero. It tells how foreman William Milner, an active member of the LNER first-aid team, gave his life in an attempt to get hold of a box of medical supplies, urgently needed for treating casualties. He entered the blazing parcels office at the height of the attack and never came back out. When his body was found, he was still clutching the box of first-aid equipment. William Milner was posthumously awarded the King's Commendation for Gallantry.

More destruction followed at the carriage works. The roundhouse took a direct hit and all of the 20 engines in there at the time suffered damage. *The Sir Ralph Wedgwood* (named after the former NER Chief General Manager) was totally destroyed when a bomb blew up in Clifton engine shed. The Leeman Road stables were also struck, necessitating the evacuation of nineteen panicking, and very dangerous, dray horses from the site. The Royal Engineers were called in to help repair the damage to the lines and the station.

Collateral damage and casualties in the vicinity of the station and its lines were substantial. 9500 houses (30% of the city's stock) were damaged or destroyed leaving 2000 people homeless. The mediaeval Guildhall and St Martin le Grand Church were badly damaged. The Bar Convent School collapsed from the blast of a direct hit, killing five nuns including the headmistress, Mother Vincent. The following day the Daily Mail reported: *'The gates of York still stand high, like the spirit of its people who, after nearly two hours of intense bombing and machine-gunning, were clearing up today. Despite rumours that 'York has been wiped off the map'*, the city and its station were quickly back to normal function. The main line reopened the afternoon after the raid although goods traffic was disrupted for longer.

Specially-constructed tank transporters built at various locations.

YORK'S RAILWAY TOURISM

As NER continued to grow at the end of the 19th century so the number of staff increased, as did the demands for office space to accommodate them. Various buildings, the redundant Scawin's Hotel for example and nearby properties, proved inadequate and temporary while 'upstairs in the old station' was hardly what was needed – either physically or from an image point of view. So it was decided that a purpose built office block Headquarters would reflect the increasing prestige and national standing of the NER, one of Britain's biggest companies. The site had been occupied by a hotel before: the 1861 *York Post Office Directory* advertises Halliwell's North Eastern Hotel as 'a First Class Hotel, near the Minster and the Museum, with excellent stabling'. No expense was spared: five million bricks were used to face the building, all hand-made in Sudbury; the other stones used are Huddlestone, Portland and Ancaster; fireproof flooring was concealed beneath black and white Belgian marble; the unique manganese bronze, copper and steel weather vane (replacing in 1922 the original) shows a NER tank locomotive Class S 4-6-0, designed to work without lubrication. The huge board room on the first floor measures 51 by 28 feet and is seventeen feet high; the walls are oak panelled and, unusually for the time, the windows were double-glazed. The biggest board room table in Britain at the time took up some of the space.

Other treasures include the corridors with their terrazzo and Roman mosaic margins and the patterned wood blocks in the offices; wrought iron balustrades, garland ceiling plasterwork and carved stone flourishes, the octagonal central hall on the first floor. This '*huge palace of business*', was completed in 1906.

Some of the plans for the HQ are displayed on the walls of what is now a 5 star hotel; this is the unique weather vane.

The glorious former NER HQ inside and out.

York has been a centre of railway management since 1840. This building, now the Headquarters of British Rail, Eastern Region, was the Head Office of the North Eastern Railway from 1906 (designed by William Bell and Horace Field).

The badges above are of the York and North Midland Railway (top), the Leeds Northern Railway (left), and the York, Newcastle and Berwick Railway (right), which formed the North Eastern Railway in 1854 and in 1923 became part of the London and North Eastern Railway.

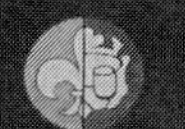

NER posters. The York Minster poster is by Fred Taylor and is from 1930.

It was the Science Museum in London – known then as the Patent Office Museum – that started the country's collection of railway artefacts by buying *Rocket* in 1866. The North Eastern Railway then opened a public railway museum in Queen's Street, York, in 1927. By the 1930s, all the other railway companies had railway-related collections ; these were combined in 1948 after Nationalisation. Under the terms of the 1968 Transport Act, a National Railway Museum was established to house the expanding collection, which was then housed in the British Transport Museum, Clapham, and in the existing York Railway Museum at Queens Street. In 1975, the celebrated National Railway Museum opened at Leeman Road in York.

It displays over 100 locomotives and 300 other items of rolling stock, most of which either ran on the railways of Great Britain or were built there. Also on the 20 acre site are many hundreds of thousands of other railway related items of social, technical, artistic and historical interest.

The museum has a unique display of royal railway vehicles, or 'palaces on wheels', indeed the best in the world. It all started when a member of staff at the London & North Western Railway works at Wolverton saved the royal saloon there from destruction. It had been used by Queen Adelaide Amelia Louisa Theresa Caroline, sister of the Duke of Saxe-Meiningen and widow of King William IV before her death in 1849. From then on many of the royal saloons of subsequent monarchs and their families have been preserved and are now in York in all their splendour.

The 8 feet 10 inch diameter railway wheels at the entrance are probably the largest locomotive wheels in existence; they were cast at Bristol in 1873 to drive 4-2-4 Tender Loco No. 40, an express passenger train of the Bristol & Exeter Railway. The wheels have been part of the National Railway Collection since 1964, and have been in their present location since 1975.

Exhibits at the old Queen Street museum.

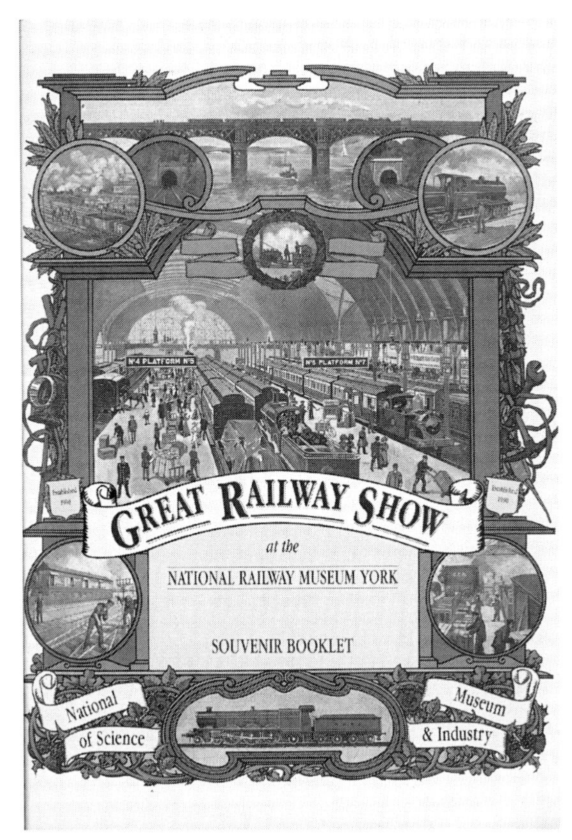

Above left: The *Great Railway Show* booklet was published in 1990.

Above right: the big wheels.

Left: on the way to the museum.

Inside the museum. © *York Press.*

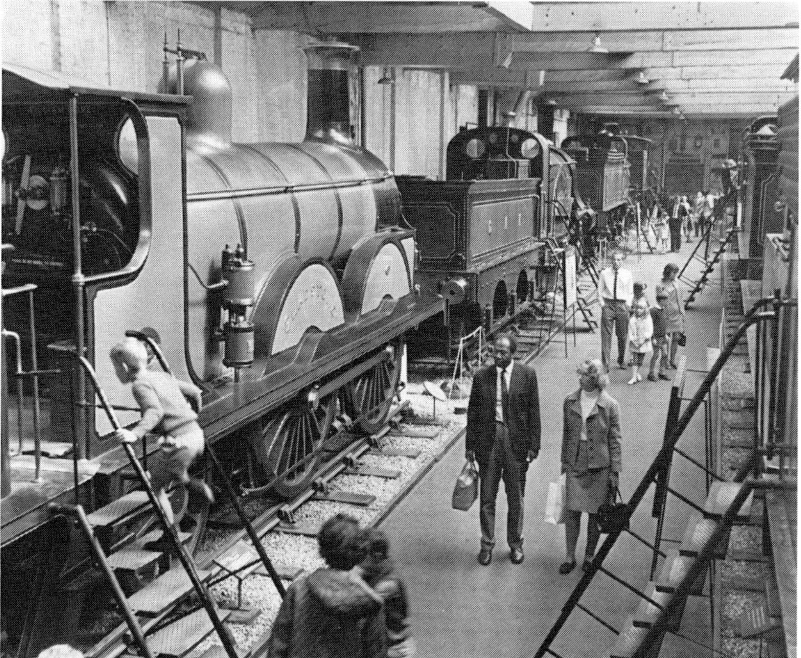

A replica of the *Iron Duke* at the national Railway Museum. © *York Press.*

A replica Stephenson's *Rocket* getting a lift at the national Railway Museum. © *York Press.*

A YORK RAILWAY MISCELLANY

DON'T DRINK

In the 1870s Henry Rowntree was a prime mover in the establishment of temperance coffee carts sited outside factories; the aim was to offer an alternative, non-alcoholic, beverage for factory workers. This was not quite as altruistic or health conscious as it might seem – sobriety went a long way to increasing productivity and reducing accidents in the Rowntree factory.

DAYLIGHT ROBBERY ON THE TRAINS

An 1868 *Punch* cartoon suggesting that the railway companies were committing daylight robbery, and featuring Dick Turpin – one of York's anti-heroes who was imprisoned, hanged and buried here.

YORK'S LISTED RAILWAY ARCHITECTURE

York has more listed railway architecture than anywhere else in Britain including the former NER offices, the Lutyens war memorial, Andrews' old railway hotel, York railway station, the old Andrew's railway station and the Royal Station (now Royal York) hotel.

Drivers, firemen and shunters at York Yard Hump in 1921. Originally published in *British Railways Magazine* (North East Region) April 1963.

A SIGNAL MEMORY

When you are leaving the station for the city from the foyer, you will see a 19th century North Eastern Railway Distant signal; this was one of the last in use on a passenger line. These signals were painted red until 1928.

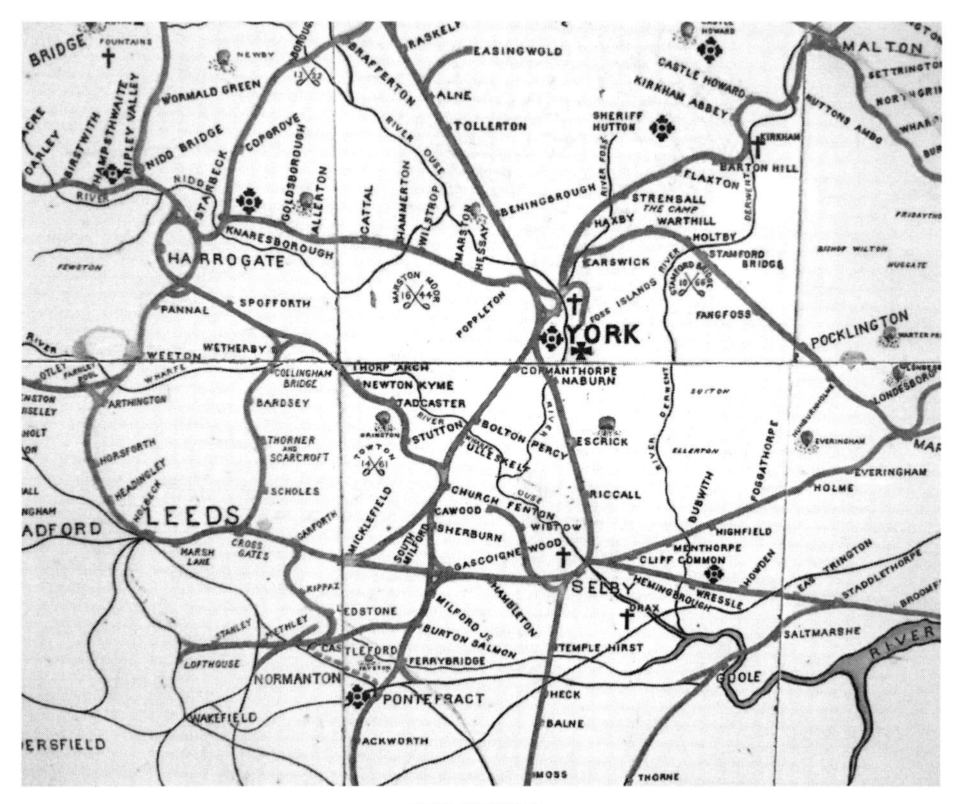

TILE MAPS

The stylish work of art that is the famous map of the NER network can be found on York Station and in the Railway Museum. The maps were made by Craven Dunill & Co of Jackfield in Shropshire and each feature 64 tiles and a moulded border.

FIRST CLASS CONSCIENCE

On one of Joseph Rowntree's train journeys , he got into a first class coach by mistake, having bought only a second class ticket. He was going to pay the difference, but the ticket inspector never came round. This troubled Rowntree greatly, so, the next time he travelled by train, he bought a first class ticket and travelled in a second class coach.

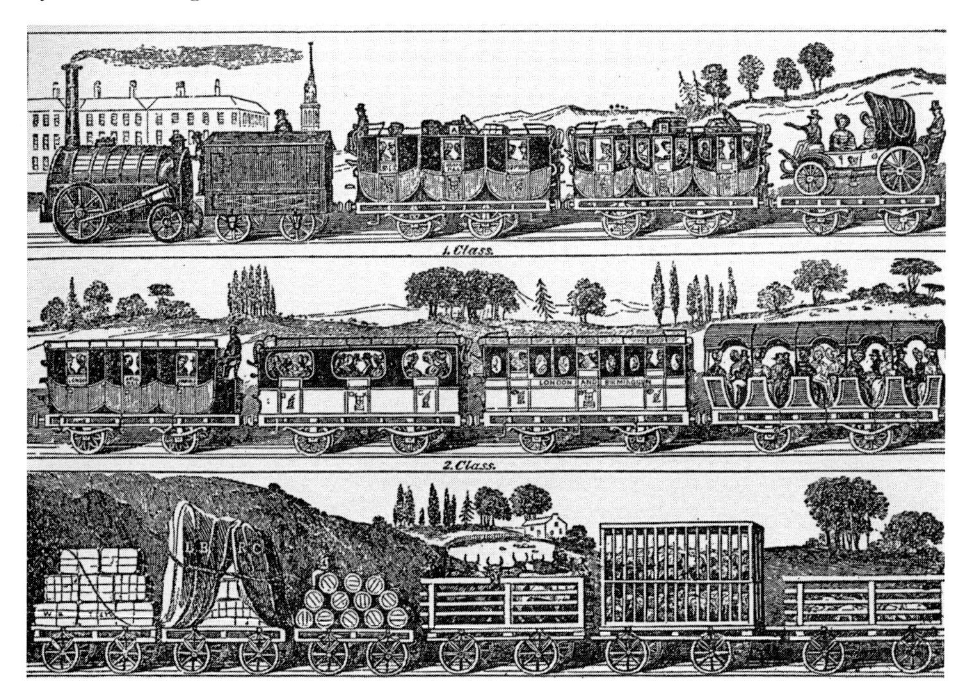

Class divisions were rigorously maintained on the railways. The Dover Railway, under Shakespeare Cliff, opened in 1844.

ROWNTREE EXCURSION GOES OFF THE RAILS

In the 1890s a work's outing to Whitby was less than successful: some of the party left the specially-chartered train at Goathland on the North York Moors planning to walk the rest of the way and meet the main group for an afternoon stroll on the beach at their destination. A rain storm intervened and diverted the walkers into a public house for shelter; when they emerged again many of them were so drunk that they had to be escorted to the station by the Whitby police.

ACCIDENTS

Luckily for York, there have been few accidents of any significance. In August 1871 a 20 wagon coal train was being propelled forwards when the coupling broke and sixteen wagons ran off the end of the staith and ended up in the river with the remaining four resting on top. On March 31st 1920, a passenger train was derailed as it entered platform 8. On August 30th 1931 a coach carrying Jack Hulbert's theatrical party from Rhyl to Scarborough was hit by the Oxfordshire en route to Sheffield. The lead dancer was seriously hurt. On August 5th 1958, a passenger train from Sunderland, 60036 *Colombo*, crashed at speed into the buffers at platform 12 ending up with the engine pointing up into the air, buffers touching the footbridge steps and the front engine bogie ripped off. No serious casualties.

There was much fear and anxiety surrounding the safety or otherwise of the railways; some of this surfaced in a salvo of satire. The carriage is the State Carriage used by the Duke of Wellington for the opening of the Liverpool and Manchester Railway. Published in *The Railway Age* by Cyril Bruyn Andrews (Country Life 1937).

HALFWAY TO EVERYWHERE

York is important because it is halfway along the East Coast main line from London to Edinburgh, 188¼ miles from King's Cross and 204½ miles from Waverley Station.

TEAROOM SQUARE

Tearoom Square takes its name from the old wooden tearoom of 1906. On the right is the octagon vestibule leading into the hotel. In between is the one survivor of the train shed's original end screens, in front of which is an entrance canopy added by William Bell also in about 1906. It saw time as a staff canteen, and after the Second World War a relics shop, railway uniform store and then the home of an extensive model railway display – *Rail Riders World* and then *York Model Railway*. Today it is the sympathetically restored Tap Inn.

Tea Room and Café in the early days.

The York Tap in Tearoom Square today...outside and...inside.

THE CHASE HOTEL: 'GATEWAY TO YORK'

Now the Marriott (since 2001) in Tadcaster Road, the Chase was part of the deal relating to the construction of York's present railway station and the Close family. Their Yorkshire and North Midland Railway house near to the cholera burial ground was in the way of the new development. To tempt the Close family to leave, in 1876 the North Eastern Railway Company agreed to build them a new house in Tadcaster Road. It became Harkers Hotel in 1927 (having moved from St Helen's Square) before being renamed the Chase Hotel in 1948. A huge saddle graced the forecourt for many years, as can be seen here.

THOMAS COOKE AND THE STEAM CAR

In 1866, Thomas Cooke branched out into three-wheeled steam cars, which reached the dizzy speed of 15 mph; however, they were outlawed by the Road Act, which prohibited vehicles that travelled in excess of 4 mph. In those days a man with a red flag had to walk in front of any vehicle not pulled by a horse. Cooke fitted his steam engine into a boat and travelled on the Ouse, free of red flags.

Similar steam contraptions were not unusual; if roads had been more developed then cars might have beaten the railways as a preferred mode of transport.

CHARLES DICKENS

On one of his visits to York in 1838, Dickens describes in his *Letters* a visit to his friend, John Camidge, organist at the Minster, who showed him round. Dickens was particularly struck by '*the deep organ's bursting heart throb through the shivering air*' and the Five Sisters Window. Dickens' story about the window appears in *Nicholas Nickleby* as the *Five Sisters of York*. The first reading was given in York at the long gone Festival Concert Rooms in Blake Street; the *Yorkshire Gazette* tells us that Dickens '*elicited unbounded applause and sent his audience home delighted*'. Mr Micawber from *David Copperfield*, too, finds his origins in York, based as he is on a Richard Chicken, a feckless character who in 1847 worked in the same railway office as Albert Dickens, Charles' railway engineer brother. Chicken was also an actor and at one time a self-styled Professor of Elocution and Lecturer on Defective Annunciation.

Dickens, of course, was himself involved in a traumatic rail accident: the Staplehurst derailment on June 9th 1865 at 3:13 pm. The South Eastern Railway Folkestone to London boat train came off the tracks while on a viaduct where a length of track had been removed during engineering works, killing ten passengers and injuring forty. Dickens was travelling with Ellen Ternan and her mother; they all survived. He gave first aid to the victims, some of whom died in his hands. Dickens was afflicted by what we would today call post traumatic stress disorder: he lost his voice for two weeks and was always nervous when travelling by train, using alternative transport if he could. Dickens died five years to the day after the accident from which he never fully recovered.

THE VICTORIA MYTH

In 1854 when Victoria, Albert and five of their children stopped off at York for a meal on the way to Balmoral, there were local complaints about the expense of such a short visit: £483 13s 7d and the meal was never eaten. Victoria got wind of the disquiet and so un-amused was she that she never visited the city again in the remaining 47 years of her reign. The Visit York website takes up the story:

> 'She had stated that this was a private visit, to be without ceremony. But the city council laid on a military display and erected stands for spectators; the Queen's temper was not improved when some of these collapsed and there was an unseemly scuffle. When the Queen eventually went to the Royal Station Hotel for her lunch, she was shocked to be presented with the bill to pay. She got up and said she would never visit York again, and never did. Whenever the Royal Train passed through York thereafter, she always made sure the blinds were firmly pulled down!'

Delightful as it is, the story is a myth. Victoria had first visited the city as a princess in 1849. She passed through York eighteen more times, getting out of the train on ten occasions.

Victoria receives a make-over in the royal carriage. © *York Press.*

Royalty goes on the rails. Published in *The Railway Age* by Cyril Bruyn Andrews (Country Life 1937).

THE GREAT YORK TRAIN ROBBERY

In October 1867 a train departed York; part of its payload was the pay for NER staff secured in the guard's van. It was noticed that the guard's van was missing when the train arrived at Strensall, the second station on the Scarborough line, after Haxby. The van was found back down the line with a dazed and confused guard. The money was, of course, missing and never recovered; no one was ever charged.

THE 'MAGNATE OF MONKGATE'

The name given to George Hudson by his rival, George Leeman. Leeman was popular because he did much good work in York building and maintaining sewers, burial grounds and streets.

'All Right'. Would you argue? Published in *The Railway Age* by Cyril Bruyn Andrews (Country Life 1937).

SCARBOROUGH BRIDGE

The Scarborough line was originally destined to bridge the Ouse at Poppleton, then at Clifton Scalp, and finally where it is now. A bridge of similar construction collapsed into the river at Chester.

NO SMOKING HERE

We tend to think of smoking restrictions as a 21st century thing. However, on June 8th 1875 Robert Bradbury defiantly lit up on one of York's platforms. He was asked to desist three times by Constable Utley, and by the assistant station master, but refused. Bradbury was later charged and fined a hefty five shillings with costs at York Guildhall.

TOM HOLTBY AND THE EDINBURGH MAIL

The railways forced the mail coaches off the road. The last run of the Edinburgh mail arrived in York in 1842 flying a black flag. The driver was the veteran Tom Holtby who died in 1863; Holtby had started out as a stable hand in The Rose & Crown in Easingwold. His success made him a wealthy man.

'MOB LAW IN YORK'

That's what the newspaper headlines screamed during the General Railway Workers strike in York on August 19th 1911: the union had called a general strike from August 16th. According to the press on August 19th 5,000 railway workers had walked out, trains were being stoned and soldiers of the York & Lancaster regiment were patrolling the city. Terry's was closed due lack of raw materials and the city magistrates were ready to read the Riot Act. The York strikers stayed out two days after the official end.

The picture (*below*) shows strikers mingling with the owners on Queen Street bridge (built 1880). On August 18th that year the general secretary of the Amalgamated Society of Railway Servants declared the first national railway strike with the words 'War is declared; the men are being called out'. It was in support of the riotous (and fatal for some) Liverpool transport strike when troops were used to attack the strikers.

'ENGINE DRIVER'S EXTRAORDINARY EXPERIENCES': TRAIN RESCUED FROM BOG BY YORK SPY

A more sanguine newspaper headline. St John Street York train driver Thomas Smith served for 45 years as an engine driver in England, Scotland, France and the USA. He was born in Naburn in 1824 but moved to France where, as a fireman and driver, he worked on the Le Havre to Paris route, among others. In 1848 he returned to Scotland where he took part in the search for an express train which was lost in a bog; the driver, stoker and guard were all killed when an engine ran off the rail 26 miles from Edinburgh and sank into the Covenshaw Bog to a depth of sixteen feet. Later he crashed his train into a passenger train at Slateford Junction near Edinburgh; after surviving a further 'two smashes in one night' he emigrated to Portland, Ohio but a serious injury in a crash near Niagara Falls forced him to return to England, and then to Rouen in 1856 where he drove trains, seemingly without incident, for a further 25 years. He was embroiled in the Franco-Prussian War and was nearly shot as a spy, and then returned to York in 1880 for some well-earned peace and quiet.

The railways brought out some of the best of British civil engineering : Brunel and the Stephensons illustrate that all too well. This is the working shaft at Kilsby Tunnel in 1837 allowing the workers access to air and light. Designed and engineered by Robert Stephenson The Kilsby Tunnel on the West Coast Main Line railway was not without its problems. It is near Kilsby in Northamptonshire five miles south-east of Rugby and is 2,432 yards long. The tunnel was opened in 1838 as a part of the London and Birmingham Railway. It is the 18th longest railway tunnel in Britain.

STATION CHRISTMAS TREES

Station Christmas trees made their first appearance in Newcastle in 1932; York's first appeared in 1937 – 20 feet high with a ten feet spread, collection boxes and coloured lights. In 1945 York raised £853 cash , £915 in 1946 with an additional £468 and £450 respectively in books and toys. In 1943 and 1944 York collected £1,000 which was used to endow a bed in the York County Hospital and dedicated by the Archbishop of York complete with plaque marking the generosity of the LNER.

TANK TRAFFIC JAM

In 1944 a US army night manoeuvre convoy was travelling along the banks of the Foss when a Sherman tank on the back of a transporter collided with the bridge carrying the Foss Islands branch line; the tank's barrel became stuck between the sleepers.

WAR ? WHAT WAR ?

Some people just won't read the papers. In August 1914 an imprudent and oblivious couple from Acomb set out on the holiday to Switzerland they had planned earlier. The railways eventually got them there, according to The *Yorkshire Evening Press*, but the return journey from a Basel in turmoil was nothing less than a nightmare. The usual seventeen hour trip to London alone took them three days and five hours. Then there was London to York...

Much of the splendour of York's Station has survived over the years, despite the efforts of the Luftwaffe. Here are four examples of details you can still see today, everyday…

The spandrels at the head of the Corinthian columns depict the coats of arms of the three companies which were merged to form the NER: York, Newcastle & Berwick Railway, the Leeds Northern Railway and the York & North Railway.

The striking clock was made by Gents of Leicester.

The spectacular sweep of the roof, looking south.

ROUNDHOUSES EXCAVATED

In 2012 the foundations of two of York's 1864 roundhouses were discovered during building work for the new training base and the new operations centre. Photo © *York Press*.

Epilogue

This book has focused on the early days of the railways in York. It is fitting that, as a kind of epilogue, we finish with a glimpse towards the future. While it may not employ the numbers of people it did in the early days, the railways continue to have a huge commercial and cultural impact on the city – not least as manifested by the unrivalled teaching and research facilities the NRM and the University of York can offer students, researchers and aficionados of railways the world over.

In 1994, the Institute of Railway Studies was launched as a joint venture between the National Railway Museum and the University of York. In 1999, *The Works* was opened, effectively expanding the museum to three times its original size. The museum won the European Museum of the Year award in 2001. The latest development is *Search Engine*, the £4 million archive and research centre that gives public access to previously unseen artwork, papers, reports, photographs and artefacts. *Search Engine* is one of the largest and richest collections of railway-related material in the world.